BTEC Apprenticeships

# BUSINESS & ADMINISTRATION

Level 2

## Assessment Workbook

KAREN GLENCROSS



www.btecapprenticeships.com

AYS LEARNING

PEARSON

Published by Pearson Education Limited, a company incorporated in England and Wales, having its registered office at Edinburgh Gate, Harlow, Essex, CM20 2JE. Registered company number: 872828

www.pearsonschoolsandfecolleges.co.uk


Edited by Kathy Peltan
Designed by Pearson Education Limited
Typeset by Phoenix Photosetting, Chatham, Kent
Cover design by Zannah Hawdon, Motif
Cover photo/illustration © Alamy Images: Oleksiy Maksymenko



First published 2011

15 14 13
10 9 8 7 6 5

**British Library Cataloguing in Publication Data**
A catalogue record for this book is available from the British Library

ISBN 978 1 446 90028 4



Printed in the UK by Ashford Colour Press Ltd.

**Acknowledgements**
The publisher would like to thank the following for their kind permission to reproduce their photographs:

(Key: b-bottom; c-centre; l-left; r-right; t-top)

Alamy Images: i love images 1, Imagestate Media Partners Limited - Impact Photos 77, INSADCO Photography 104r, Julie Thompson 71t, PhotoAlto 26; Corbis: 29, Image Source 103; Getty Images: Imagebank 87c, Stone 2; iStockphoto: Jacob Wackerhausen 83, Lisa Gagne 13, 17, Maridav 104l, Radu Razvan 110; Masterfile UK Ltd: 105l, George Remington 105r; Pearson Education Ltd: 55; Gareth Boden 84; Plainpicture Ltd: Johner 98; Rex Features: Nick White / Mood Board 75, 91; Shutterstock.com: Andreja Donko 70b, calmacanul 71b, lightpoet 35, 44, Martin Novak 8, Morgan Lane Photography 38, Norman Chan 70t, Stephen Coburn 87t, trek and shoot 115, Yuri Arcurs 87b

All other images © Pearson Education

Every effort has been made to trace the copyright holders and we apologise in advance for any unintentional omissions. We would be pleased to insert the appropriate acknowledgement in any subsequent edition of this publication.



Additional support for using this Assessment Workbook is available from www.btecapprenticeshipworkbooks.co.uk

**Username:** busadmin2
**Password:** ba2learn

# BTEC APPRENTICESHIP LEVEL 2 BUSINESS & ADMINISTRATION

| | |
|---|---|
| Apprentice name | |
| Apprentice number | |
| Assessor name | |
| Training provider | |
| Employer | |



| | |
|---|---|
| The candidate has successfully completed all relevant sections of the BTEC Apprenticeship Assessment Workbook | |
| **Assessor's signature:** | **Date:** |
| I confirm that all the work submitted is my own and that all sources of information have been fully acknowledged | |
| **Apprentice's signature:** | **Date:** |

# INTRODUCTION TO YOUR BTEC APPRENTICESHIP

An Apprenticeship is a work-based qualification. While you are working for your employer and developing your skills and knowledge in the workplace, you will also have regular contact with an **assessor**. Your assessor will support you in your learning and assessment, possibly sometimes at a local college or training centre.

There is a glossary on page xiv explaining key terms that you will come across frequently during your Apprenticeship. These words appear in **bold** when they first come up in this introduction.

Your Level 2 BTEC Apprenticeship in Business & Administration may consist of the following qualifications:

- NVQ Level 2 Certificate Business & Administration
- BTEC Level 2 Certificate Business & Administration
- BTEC WorkSkills for Effective Learning and Employment
- Functional Skills at Level 1 in English, mathematics and ICT
- OR Key Skills at Level 1 in Communication, Application of Number and ICT (only until September 2012)
- OR Essential Skills Wales in Communication, Application of Number and ICT (if you are based in Wales)
- Employment Responsibilities and Rights
- Personal, Learning and Thinking Skills (in England only)

All of these qualifications, apart from Functional Skills and part of Key Skills, can be assessed through practical work-based activities, evidence of what you do in your day-to-day job, and discussions and observations with your assessor.

## ASSESSMENT

This Assessment Workbook will help you make the most of the different assessment options that are available for your Apprenticeship. You may be assessed through:

- work tasks that let you demonstrate your competence
- observations of you completing work tasks
- discussions with your assessor that demonstrate your knowledge and understanding
- written evidence, for example completed Knowledge and Understanding pages from this Assessment Workbook.

Any assessment work will need to be recorded for your **portfolio**. Your assessor will advise you of the best methods of recording this evidence. Because you may work with confidential information, your portfolio should contain the location of any naturally occurring workplace evidence (such as letters or reports) rather than a copy of the documents themselves.

Your assessor will let you know if the BTEC Certificate will be assessed using onscreen tests. If you are being assessed onscreen, you may find the interactive quizzes provided at www.btecapprenticeshipworkbooks.co.uk help prepare you for the test.

Your assessor will help you select the units of the different qualifications that best suit your needs and the needs of your employer. This Assessment Workbook does not cover every optional unit in the qualification, so your assessor will let you know which sections of the Workbook are most relevant for your Apprenticeship.

As part of your Apprenticeship, you may need to pass the Functional Skills qualifications listed opposite. These are assessed through timed tests, which may be paper-based or onscreen. Your assessor will advise you of when you will sit these and will help you prepare for the assessment. You can find practice assessment activities at www.btecapprenticeshipworkbooks.co.uk. If you are taking Key Skills or Essential Skills Wales instead, your assessor will discuss with you when and how you will complete this assessment.

## THE ROLE OF YOUR EMPLOYER

During your BTEC Apprenticeship, your employer needs to provide you with:

- enough time to allow you to complete your Apprenticeship work
- opportunities to demonstrate the necessary skills in your workplace
- a mentor to help provide informal training and support
- a wage.

In addition, your employer (or your colleagues) may support you in completing your Apprenticeship through:

- providing witness statements that can be used as evidence for your Apprenticeship
- additional training where you need to develop your skills and knowledge further
- support and guidance if you have any human resources issues.

## THE ROLE OF YOUR ASSESSOR

Your assessor will support you in completing your BTEC Apprenticeship. He or she will visit you at your workplace and discuss the Apprenticeship with you to make sure qualifications are suitable for your needs and job role, and that you fully understand what you will need to learn and do during the Apprenticeship programme.

During your Apprenticeship, your assessor needs to:

- make sure you understand how you will be assessed and what you will be assessed on
- give you good notice of each time they visit you at your workplace, and what you need to have completed in preparation for the visit
- discuss your work and your job role with your employer and colleagues to gather additional evidence for your portfolio.

In addition, your assessor may recommend supporting resources, such as textbooks or e-learning, that you need to use during the course of the Apprenticeship to help you build your knowledge and skills.

## YOUR ROLE

You are responsible for both carrying out the job that your employer is paying you to do and for completing your Apprenticeship. Your responsibilities to your employer are:

- to do the work required of you to a satisfactory standard
- to keep your employer informed of how you are progressing through the Apprenticeship
- to meet the general requirements of an employee at your workplace (for example, to turn up on time).

You also have responsibilities to your assessor. Your assessor will need you to:

- inform your employer of the dates when your assessor is visiting you at your workplace
- complete the work required of you by the date agreed, and if you are unable to do so, keep your assessor informed of your progress
- attend any training organised by your training provider
- keep them informed of the work activities you are planning to carry out on the dates of your assessor visits – if you will not be in the workplace on that day, tell your assessor as soon as possible so they can reschedule the visit
- make sure your work is your own and that you indicate the original source of any information or wording that you have found somewhere else (for example, on the Internet).

# HOW TO USE THIS BTEC APPRENTICESHIP ASSESSMENT WORKBOOK

This BTEC Apprenticeship Assessment Workbook has been designed to support you and your assessor in completing your BTEC Apprenticeship. It helps you to prove your knowledge, understanding and skills, and identify evidence that will demonstrate your competence and go towards achieving your Apprenticeship.

As you will be submitting this Assessment Workbook to your assessor as evidence for your Apprenticeship, you need to make sure you keep it safe and update it regularly.

## WHAT THE ASSESSMENT WORKBOOK COVERS

Your assessor will discuss your Apprenticeship with you and will identify a number of units that will be relevant to you and your job role. This Assessment Workbook covers the mandatory units and a selection of optional units to complete the qualifications that make up the BTEC Apprenticeship.

| | Credits | Mandatory/ Optional |
|---|---|---|
| **BTEC Level 2 Certificate Business & Administration** | | |
| **Unit 1:** Principles of personal responsibilities and working in a business environment | 4 | M |
| **Unit 2:** Principles of providing administrative services | 4 | M |
| **Unit 3:** Principles of managing information and producing documents | 3 | M |
| **Unit 7:** Building working relationships with customers | 2 | O |
| **NVQ Level 2 Certificate Business & Administration** | | |
| **Unit 1:** Manage own performance in a business environment | 2 | M |
| **Unit 2:** Improve own performance in a business environment | 2 | M |
| **Unit 3:** Work in a business environment | 2 | M |
| **Unit 4:** Communicate in a business environment | 3 | M |
| **Unit 6:** Work with other people in a business environment | 3 | O |
| **Unit 8:** Produce documents in a business environment | 4 | O |
| **Unit 24:** Make and receive telephone calls | 3 | O |
| **Unit 25:** Use electronic message systems | 1 | O |
| **Unit 26:** Use diary systems | 3 | O |
| **Unit 31:** Provide reception services | 3 | O |
| **Unit 34:** Deliver, monitor and evaluate customer service to external customers | 3 | O |

| | Credits | Mandatory/ Optional |
|---|---|---|
| **Unit 36:** Research information | 4 | O |
| **Unit 37:** Store and retrieve information | 3 | O |
| **Unit 38:** Archive information | 2 | O |
| **Unit 43:** Use office equipment | 4 | O |
| **Unit 52:** Use occupational and safety guidelines when using keyboards | 2 | O |
| **Level 2 BTEC WorkSkills for Effective Learning and Employment** | | |
| **Unit 1:** Preparing for an Apprenticeship | 1 | M |
| **Unit 2:** Understanding employment responsibilities and rights | 3 | O |
| **Unit 5:** Understanding the employing organisation | 2 | O |
| **Unit 6:** Understanding employment rights and responsibilities | 2 | O |
| **Unit 7:** Using enquiry and investigative techniques to solve problems (CT/IE) | 1 | O |
| **Unit 8:** Participating in team work (EP/TW) | 1 | O |
| **Unit 9:** Manage own learning (RL/SM) | 1 | O |

The Assessment Workbook also covers the Employment Rights and Responsibilities (ERR) and Personal, Learning and Thinking Skills (PLTS) requirements set by the Standard Setting Body for an Apprenticeship in Business & Administration. Your assessor also has separate information showing how you can prove your basic skills if you are taking either Key Skills or Essential Skills Wales qualifications.

## USING THE BTEC APPRENTICESHIP ASSESSMENT WORKBOOK

The Assessment Workbook contains a mixture of activities and guidance, which combine assessment criteria from these different qualifications and involve real work activities related to your day-to-day job. Your assessor will suggest which activities and sections you should complete and read at each point of your Apprenticeship. Use the activities and guidance to create or collect evidence, and to prepare for observations and professional discussions when your assessor visits you in your workplace.

In the margins of the Assessment Workbook you will see references to the assessment criteria covered (or partially covered) by each activity. The following abbreviations have been used:

- BTEC = BTEC Level 2 Certificate
- NVQ = NVQ Level 2 Certificate
- WorkSkills = WorkSkills for Effective Learning and Employment
- PLTS = Personal, Learning and Thinking Skills

The different activities and information in the Assessment Workbook are as follows.

## KNOWLEDGE AND UNDERSTANDING TASKS

Complete these tasks to produce evidence of your knowledge and understanding of the different parts of your Apprenticeship. This may involve talking to your colleagues or manager, and will normally be completed before your assessor visits you in your workplace. Before each assessor visit, your assessor will discuss with you which activities they want you to complete.

You will also find electronic versions of these tasks online at www.btecapprenticeshipworkbooks.co.uk ready for you to type into and save. Your assessor will discuss with you how to complete the tasks.

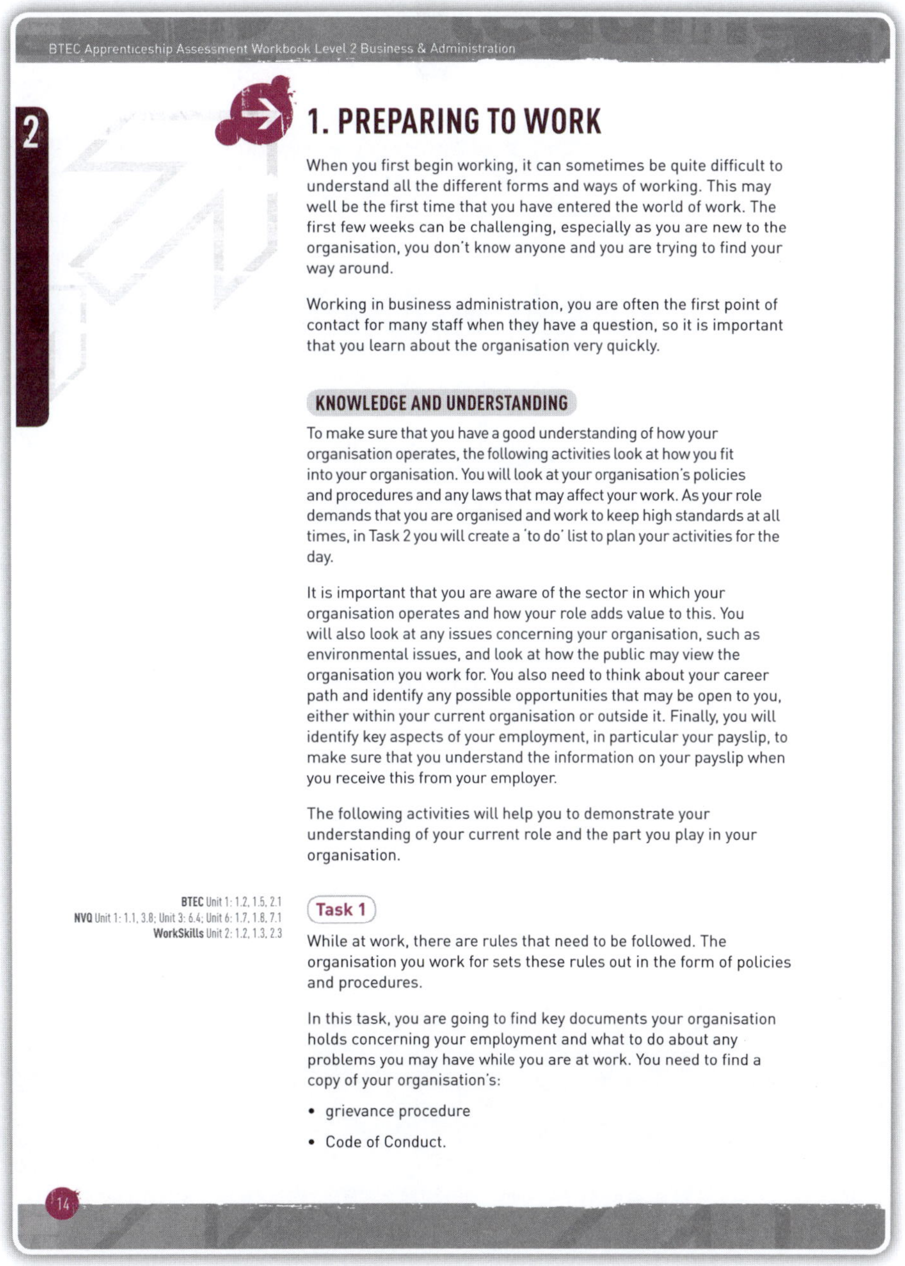

BTEC Apprenticeship Assessment Workbook Level 2 Business & Administration

2

### 1. PREPARING TO WORK

When you first begin working, it can sometimes be quite difficult to understand all the different forms and ways of working. This may well be the first time that you have entered the world of work. The first few weeks can be challenging, especially as you are new to the organisation, you don't know anyone and you are trying to find your way around.

Working in business administration, you are often the first point of contact for many staff when they have a question, so it is important that you learn about the organisation very quickly.

#### KNOWLEDGE AND UNDERSTANDING

To make sure that you have a good understanding of how your organisation operates, the following activities look at how you fit into your organisation. You will look at your organisation's policies and procedures and any laws that may affect your work. As your role demands that you are organised and work to keep high standards at all times, in Task 2 you will create a 'to do' list to plan your activities for the day.

It is important that you are aware of the sector in which your organisation operates and how your role adds value to this. You will also look at any issues concerning your organisation, such as environmental issues, and look at how the public may view the organisation you work for. You also need to think about your career path and identify any possible opportunities that may be open to you, either within your current organisation or outside it. Finally, you will identify key aspects of your employment, in particular your payslip, to make sure that you understand the information on your payslip when you receive this from your employer.

The following activities will help you to demonstrate your understanding of your current role and the part you play in your organisation.

**BTEC** Unit 1: 1.2, 1.5, 2.1
**NVQ** Unit 1: 1.1, 3.8; Unit 3: 6.4; Unit 6: 1.7, 1.8, 7.1
**WorkSkills** Unit 2: 1.2, 1.3, 2.3

**Task 1**

While at work, there are rules that need to be followed. The organisation you work for sets these rules out in the form of policies and procedures.

In this task, you are going to find key documents your organisation holds concerning your employment and what to do about any problems you may have while you are at work. You need to find a copy of your organisation's:

- grievance procedure
- Code of Conduct.

14

## EVIDENCE GATHERING

Use this information to identify where what you do in your everyday work can form part of the evidence you can submit for your Apprenticeship. This evidence needs to fit certain requirements, which are listed here, so make sure you check your evidence against these before including it in your portfolio.

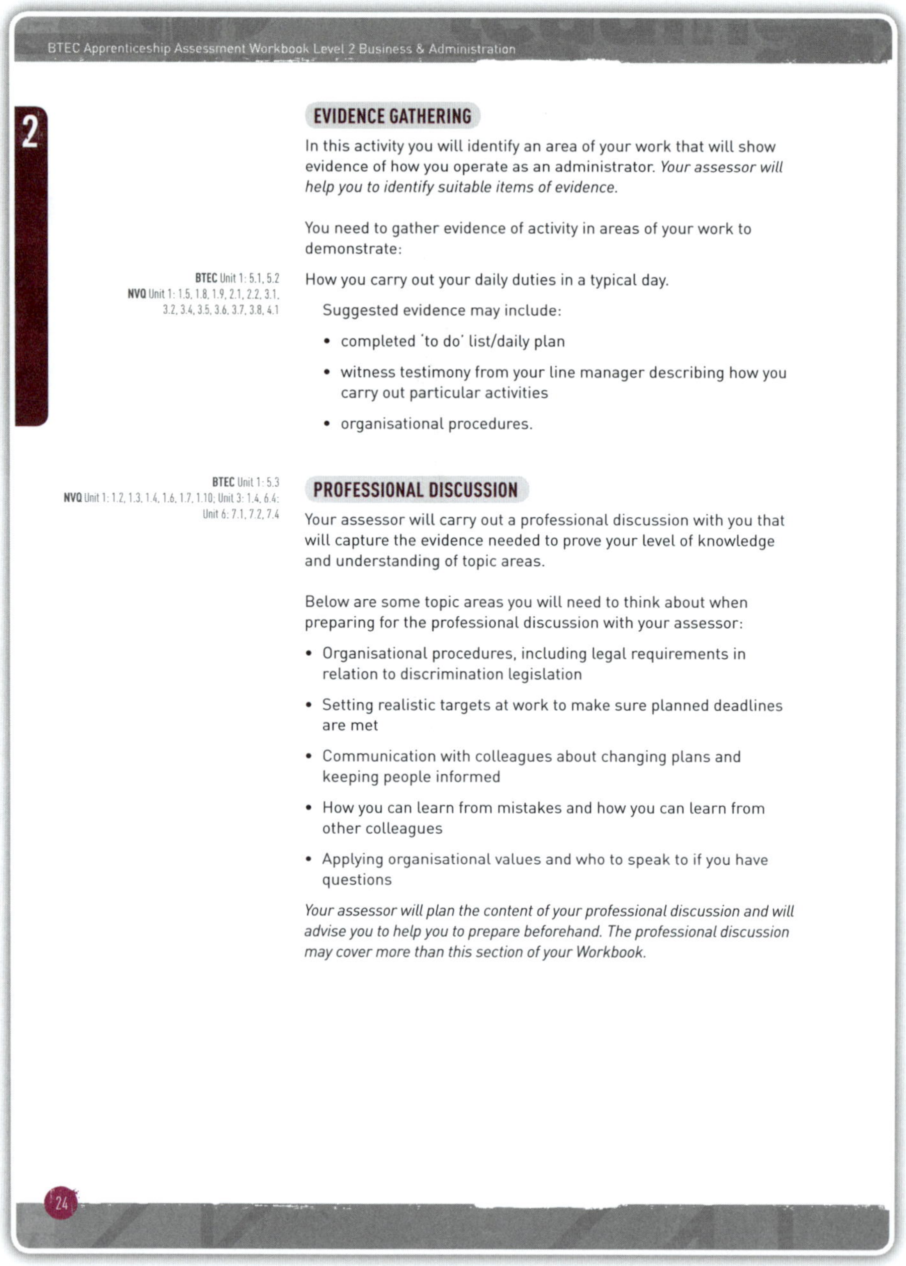



2

### EVIDENCE GATHERING

In this activity you will identify an area of your work that will show evidence of how you operate as an administrator. *Your assessor will help you to identify suitable items of evidence.*

You need to gather evidence of activity in areas of your work to demonstrate:

**BTEC** Unit 1: 5.1, 5.2
**NVQ** Unit 1: 1.5, 1.8, 1.9, 2.1, 2.2, 3.1, 3.2, 3.4, 3.5, 3.6, 3.7, 3.8, 4.1

How you carry out your daily duties in a typical day.

Suggested evidence may include:

- completed 'to do' list/daily plan
- witness testimony from your line manager describing how you carry out particular activities
- organisational procedures.

**BTEC** Unit 1: 5.3
**NVQ** Unit 1: 1.2, 1.3, 1.4, 1.6, 1.7, 1.10; Unit 3: 1.4, 6.4; Unit 6: 7.1, 7.2, 7.4

### PROFESSIONAL DISCUSSION

Your assessor will carry out a professional discussion with you that will capture the evidence needed to prove your level of knowledge and understanding of topic areas.

Below are some topic areas you will need to think about when preparing for the professional discussion with your assessor:

- Organisational procedures, including legal requirements in relation to discrimination legislation
- Setting realistic targets at work to make sure planned deadlines are met
- Communication with colleagues about changing plans and keeping people informed
- How you can learn from mistakes and how you can learn from other colleagues
- Applying organisational values and who to speak to if you have questions

*Your assessor will plan the content of your professional discussion and will advise you to help you to prepare beforehand. The professional discussion may cover more than this section of your Workbook.*

## PUTTING IT INTO PRACTICE

These sections prepare you for **observations**, when your assessor may want to observe you at work during their visits. Your assessor may also ask you questions about what you're doing to check your understanding, so make sure you read through the preparation notes provided here. Your assessor will discuss with you which of these sections you should read, depending on which work activities you are going to be carrying out when they next visit you at your workplace.

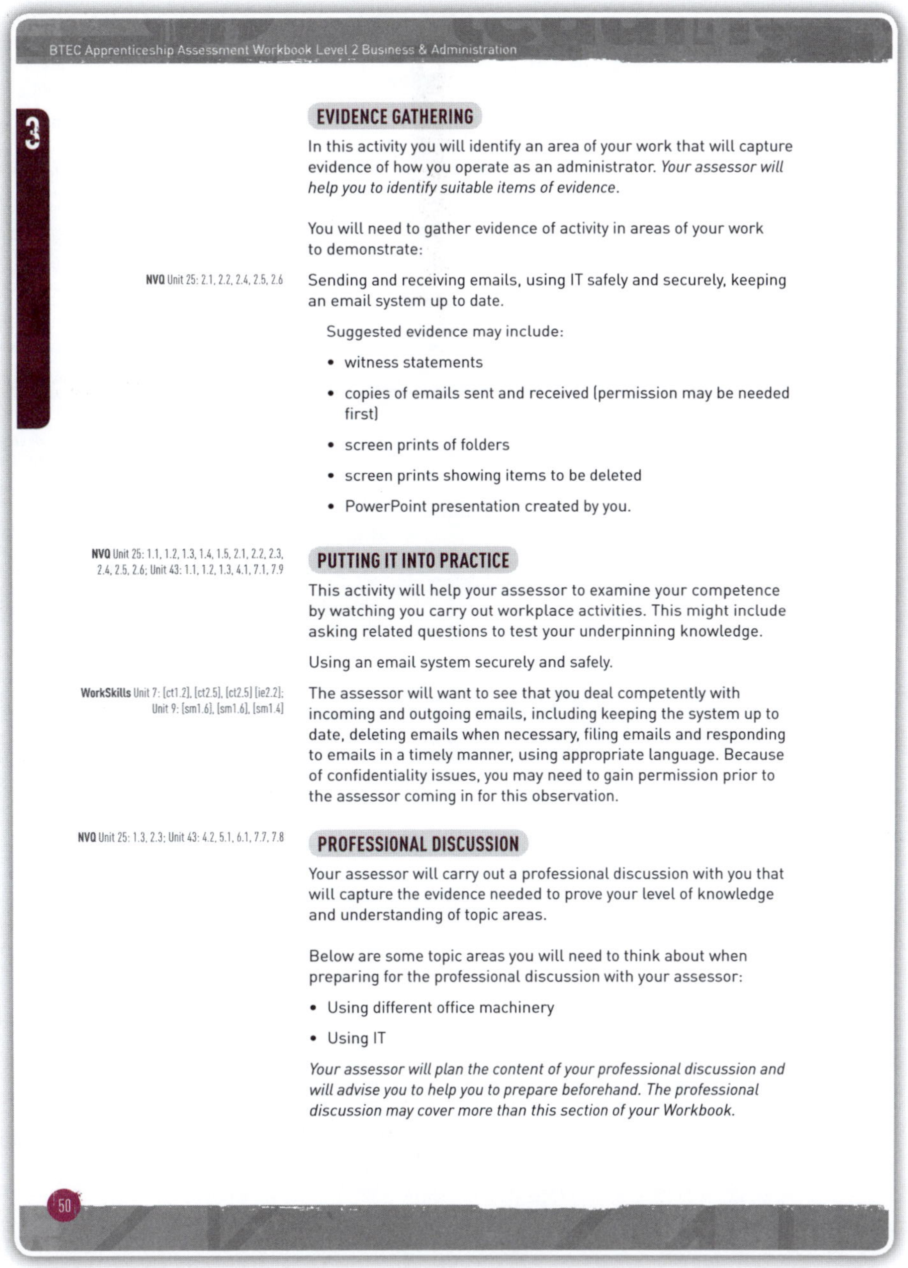

BTEC Apprenticeship Assessment Workbook Level 2 Business & Administration

3

### EVIDENCE GATHERING

In this activity you will identify an area of your work that will capture evidence of how you operate as an administrator. *Your assessor will help you to identify suitable items of evidence.*

You will need to gather evidence of activity in areas of your work to demonstrate:

**NVQ** Unit 25: 2.1, 2.2, 2.4, 2.5, 2.6

Sending and receiving emails, using IT safely and securely, keeping an email system up to date.

Suggested evidence may include:

- witness statements
- copies of emails sent and received (permission may be needed first)
- screen prints of folders
- screen prints showing items to be deleted
- PowerPoint presentation created by you.

**NVQ** Unit 25: 1.1, 1.2, 1.3, 1.4, 1.5, 2.1, 2.2, 2.3, 2.4, 2.5, 2.6; Unit 43: 1.1, 1.2, 1.3, 4.1, 7.1, 7.9

### PUTTING IT INTO PRACTICE

This activity will help your assessor to examine your competence by watching you carry out workplace activities. This might include asking related questions to test your underpinning knowledge.

Using an email system securely and safely.

**WorkSkills** Unit 7: [ct1.2], [ct2.5], [ct2.5] [ie2.2]; Unit 9: [sm1.6], [sm1.6], [sm1.4]

The assessor will want to see that you deal competently with incoming and outgoing emails, including keeping the system up to date, deleting emails when necessary, filing emails and responding to emails in a timely manner, using appropriate language. Because of confidentiality issues, you may need to gain permission prior to the assessor coming in for this observation.

**NVQ** Unit 25: 1.3, 2.3; Unit 43: 4.2, 5.1, 6.1, 7.7, 7.8

### PROFESSIONAL DISCUSSION

Your assessor will carry out a professional discussion with you that will capture the evidence needed to prove your level of knowledge and understanding of topic areas.

Below are some topic areas you will need to think about when preparing for the professional discussion with your assessor:

- Using different office machinery
- Using IT

*Your assessor will plan the content of your professional discussion and will advise you to help you to prepare beforehand. The professional discussion may cover more than this section of your Workbook.*

50

## PROFESSIONAL DISCUSSION

Your assessor will carry out, and record, **professional discussions** with you to check your knowledge, understanding and skills. They may combine the professional discussions from more than one section of the Assessment Workbook if they want to discuss several topics at the same time. These sections will help you prepare for discussion when your assessor visits you at your workplace.



4

questions to check your understanding of the company policies and procedures in respect of health and safety, and security.

**BTEC** Unit 2: 9.3
**NVQ** Unit 24: 1.2, 1.6, 1.8; 2.2, 2.3, 2.6; Unit 31: 4.10

### PROFESSIONAL DISCUSSION

Your assessor will carry out a professional discussion with you that will capture the evidence needed to prove your level of knowledge and understanding of topic areas.

Below are some topic areas you will need to think about when preparing for the professional discussion with your assessor:

- The purpose of telephone calls
- Summarising telephone calls
- Communication structures
- Confidentiality and telephone calls
- Other duties of a receptionist

*Your assessor will plan the content of your professional discussion and will advise you to help you to prepare beforehand. The professional discussion may cover more than this section of your Workbook.*

#### Discussion process

The discussion process offers you the chance to show that you are comfortable working on reception and have a grasp of the issues that may arise while working in that area.

To prepare for your professional discussion, you should think about how you could answer questions such as the following:

- Why is it important to know the purpose of a telephone call before you make it?
- Why should you try to summarise a telephone call?
- What is the communication structure in your organisation?
- What are the confidentiality issues around telephone callers and working on a reception desk?
- During a quiet period on reception, what would you do?

## www.btecapprenticeshipworkbooks.co.uk

There is a website that accompanies this Assessment Workbook, which contains the following additional support for you:

- interactive revision activities to help you prepare for onscreen assessment for the BTEC Level 2 Certificate. (Your assessor will discuss and agree with you if you are going to use this kind of assessment.) You can, of course, also use these revision quizzes to check your knowledge if you are not using onscreen assessment.
- electronic copies of the Knowledge and Understanding tasks from the Assessment Workbook that you can complete and save. You may need the latest version of Adobe Acrobat Reader to use these. The free software can be downloaded from http://get.adobe.com/reader/
- practice Functional Skills activities to help you develop your skills and prepare you for the test.

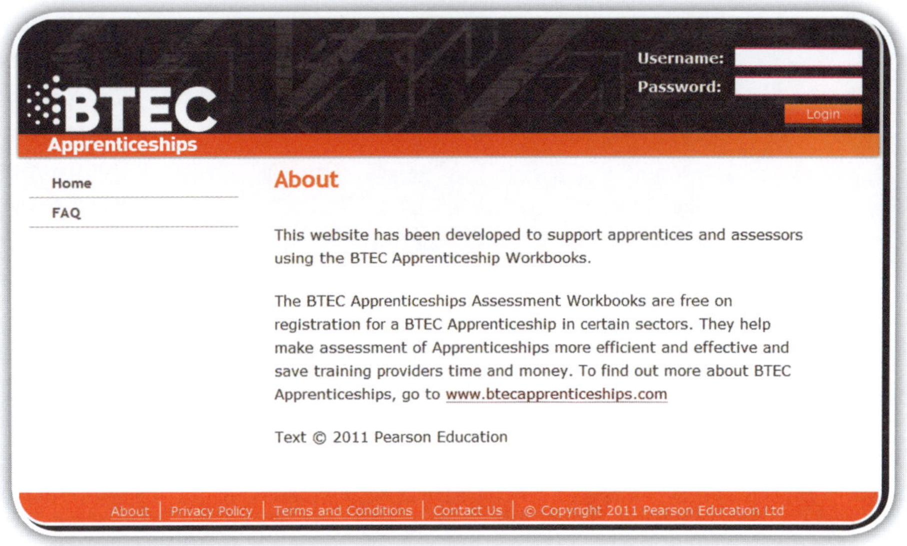


To log on to this website:

1. Go to www.btecapprenticeshipworkbooks.co.uk
2. In the login box on the top-right corner of your screen, use the following login details:

   **Username:** busadmin2
   **Password:** ba2learn

3. Click on "Login". You will then be able to select the support materials you want to use.

# GLOSSARY

Below is a list of key terms that you will come across frequently in your Apprenticeship and the BTEC Apprenticeship Assessment Workbook.

**Assessment criteria** statements within a unit of a qualification describing the standards by which your skills or knowledge will be measured.

**Assessor** the person from your training provider who will visit you in your workplace; their role is to support you through your Apprenticeship and to assess your performance and knowledge.

**Competence** your skills and abilities in performing your work; competence means having the necessary knowledge and skills for your role.

**Evidence** Anything that demonstrates you have the knowledge, understanding and skills specified in the assessment criteria.

**Learning outcome** statements within a unit of a qualification describing what you will have learned or be able to do once you have completed part of a unit.

**Observation** your assessor will watch you carrying out practical activities and parts of your job in order to judge your competence and will then keep a formal record of your performance.

**Portfolio** you and your assessor will need to record and organise the items of evidence you gather during your apprenticeship; a portfolio helps you to keep everything together and allows you to monitor your progress over time. Some training providers use paper-based portfolios, while others use e-portfolios, in which your evidence is recorded and stored digitally.

**Professional discussion** a structured conversation with your assessor that allows you to demonstrate your understanding of work practice or procedures and may also enable you to provide evidence of knowledge or competence.

**Training provider** a college or private training organisation responsible for assessing your competence in your workplace and, where necessary, for delivering additional training to develop your knowledge and skills.

**Witness statement** a statement that can support your evidence of competence, from a person who is qualified to make comments about your performance (for example, your manager). It must include: a description of the activity you have carried out; how it relates to the assessment criteria; when and in what context the activity was carried out.

# 1

**During this Induction visit, your assessor will check that you have settled into your Apprenticeship programme and into the area that you are working in. Your assessor will also check that you are comfortable with how the Apprenticeship programme will work, and you will be able to introduce your assessor to key people in your organisation who may be able to help you complete your programme successfully.**

**Your Apprenticeship induction is a process designed to give you the opportunity to show your knowledge and understanding of the following:**

### 1. You and your employment

Topic areas that may be discussed include:

- Employment contract terms
- Employer and employee responsibilities
- Employment legislation
- Progression plans after completing the Apprenticeship

This is the first section in your journey through your Apprenticeship programme and will form the first visit that your assessor makes to your workplace.

This section introduces you to your role as an administrator in your organisation. You will need to collect various documents relating to your employment, as well as planning your route through the programme.

Your assessor may wish to carry out an observation of you in the workplace and will also want to speak with your line manager/supervisor, although this may not take place during the Induction visit. It is normal practice for your assessor to have a meeting with your manager, and is nothing to worry about.

1

# 1. YOU AND YOUR EMPLOYMENT

The activities in this section will take you through the key documents concerning your employment, to make sure that you are fully aware of their existence and what they mean. You will also take an in-depth look at how your Apprenticeship programme is structured and learn how your assessor and line manager/supervisor will provide support to make sure that you achieve this programme.

## KNOWLEDGE AND UNDERSTANDING

This section takes you through a series of activities that focus on your knowledge of key documents concerning the world of work, and your own employment. This section also explains where you can get help and advice during your employment and allows you to plan your Apprenticeship programme so that you can set yourself realistic goals.

**BTEC** Unit 1: 1.1, 1.3
**WorkSkills** Unit 2: 2.1

### Task 1

Your contract of employment is a key document given to you when you begin your role in an organisation. You must remember that, although your employer has responsibilities concerning your employment, you have responsibilities too. It is your responsibility to understand your contract of employment and to complete your duties following company rules and procedures.

You are going to take an in-depth look at your own contract of employment to make sure that you understand what it contains. You must remember that no two employment contracts of employment are identical – they will contain the same basic information, but each contract will have some details that specifically relate to that individual employee.

*Why is important to take the time to read the terms of your contract of employment?*

The table below contains the most important aspects of your contract of employment. Read through the list and find where the information is contained on your contract. Then complete the table with the correct information. The first line has been completed for you as an example.

| Contract of employment terms | What does your contract of employment say about this term? |
|---|---|
| Job title | *Administration Assistant* |
| Payment/ salary | |
| Your working hours | |
| Holiday/annual leave | |
| Sick pay arrangements | |
| Special leave arrangements | |
| Disciplinary and grievance procedures | |
| Notice period and termination of contract | |

There will be other information contained in your contract that you may feel is important. You can add to this list if you wish.

1

**BTEC** Unit 1: 1.1

## Task 2

Your contract of employment is a legal document and both you and your employer have responsibilities.

Read the following questions about rights and responsibilities and write in the space below where and how you would find out further information:

1. You want to visit relatives in New Zealand next year and want to take extra paid leave. Are you able to save or transfer holidays from one year to the next?

2. You wake up feeling too ill to go into work one morning. What should you do?

3. If you deliberately ignored the terms of your contract of employment, what do you think the consequences would be?

**WorkSkills** Unit 1: 2.2, 2.3, 3.2

## Task 3

In the first part of this task, you are going to write an action plan, giving details of the timescale you intend to take to complete your Apprenticeship programme. In the second part of this task you will start planning what you will do after this programme – you may wish to include several options in this section.

1. A suggested format could be the following, although you can use your own format if you wish.

| Unit(s) | Topics | Review date | To be completed by | Achieved? |
| --- | --- | --- | --- | --- |
| | | | | |
| | | | | |
| | | | | |
| | | | | |
| | | | | |
| | | | | |
| | | | | |
| | | | | |
| | | | | |
| | | | | |
| | | | | |
| | | | | |
| | | | | |
| | | | | |

2. An administrator needs to be organised. In the space below, describe:

   a. why you think it is important to be organised

   b. why an action plan may help you to be organised.

3. It is important to look forward and think about what you will do once you have completed this Apprenticeship. The following table gives you three areas into which you could progress. In the spaces underneath the headings, compare the routes and give your reasons for either wanting, or not wanting, to follow that route.

| **I would like to progress to employment** | **I would like to progress to full-time education** | **I would like to progress to Level 3 Apprenticeship** |
|---|---|---|
| | | |
| | | |
| | | |

BTEC Unit 1: 1.3, 1.4

## Task 4

While you are at work, you may have access to representative bodies that look after the welfare and well-being of employees. This could be a trade union, or similar body.

In this task, you are going to investigate how employee support through representative bodies is carried out in your organisation. You may need to ask your line manager/supervisor for guidance in order to carry out this task.

1. Complete the table below by answering the questions.

| Facts about representative bodies | Further details |
|---|---|
| What is/are the name(s) of the representative body(ies)? | |
| Who does/do this/these body(ies) represent? | |
| What do you have to do to join? | |
| Is there a cost involved? | |
| What help and support can this/ these body(ies) give you? | |
| Are there any benefits to joining? | |
| Is it compulsory to join? | |
| Is there a representative body on site? | |

2. If you do identify a representative body in your organisation, would you join it and why?

3. If your organisation has a representative body, what benefits would there be to you as an employee to be part of it?

**BTEC** Unit 1: 1.2, 1.5
**WorkSkills** Unit 2: 1.2, 1.4

## Task 5

Before completing this task, find a copy of your organisation's policy/procedures relating to:

- equality and diversity.

1. Using the internet, your organisation's policies and procedures, and other suitable sources of information, identify what the following Acts cover in terms of equality *and* diversity and then say how your organisation deals with the issues. Write your answers in the table opposite.

*You can use the internet to research information on employment legislation.*

| Name and date of Act | What does this mean? | How does your organisation deal with the issue? |
|---|---|---|
| The Sex Discrimination Act 1975 (as amended) | | |
| The Race Relations Act 1976 (as amended) | | |
| The Employment Equality (Sexual Orientation) Regulations 2003 | | |
| The Employment Equality (Religion or Belief) Regulations 2003 | | |
| The Disability Discrimination Act 1995 (as amended) | | |
| The Gender Recognition Act 2004 | | |
| The Equality Act 2010 | | |

There are a number of other pieces of legislation that you must be aware of.

Before you attempt the remainder of the task, find a copy of the following in your workplace:

- the policy/procedure for health and safety for your organisation (this may be kept electronically on a shared drive or intranet site).

2. The table below looks at some of the aspects of your employment that have relevant legislation. Using a suitable form of research, such as the internet, books, and so on, identify the laws that cover the areas of your employment listed in the table below:

| **Area of your employment** | **State the piece of legislation or law that covers this** |
| --- | --- |
| Your health and safety at work | |
| Maternity, paternity and parental leave guidelines | |
| Your working hours | |
| Pay and pensions | |
| Equal pay | |

**WorkSkills** Unit 1: 1.1, 1.2, 1.3, 2.1, 2.2, 3.1, 3.2



## PROFESSIONAL DISCUSSION

Your assessor will carry out a professional discussion with you that will capture the evidence needed to prove your level of knowledge and understanding of topic areas.

Below are some topic areas you will need to think about when preparing for the professional discussion with your assessor:

- Being organised in your role
- Understanding your Apprenticeship Framework
- Creating targets
- Deadlines and their importance

*Your assessor will plan the content of your professional discussion and will advise you to help you to prepare beforehand. The professional discussion may cover more than this section of your Workbook.*

### Discussion process

The discussion process offers you the chance to show that you have a good understanding of your employment and your Apprenticeship. It is important that you take responsibility in many different areas and this discussion will give you an opportunity to show this.

To prepare for your professional discussion, you should think about how you could answer questions such as the following:

- Why do you think meeting deadlines is important?
- Do you know how you will be assessed during your Apprenticeship?
- Which units are you studying and why?
- What is the purpose of setting targets for yourself?
- What do you see yourself doing after completion of this Apprenticeship?

The table on page 12 has been created to allow you and your assessor to look at the units of the Framework you are going to complete and identify how each unit will be assessed. This will give you a greater understanding of how your Apprenticeship will work and allow you to plan your progression through the qualifications.

1

| Unit | Unit name | How will this be assessed? |
|---|---|---|
| 1 | Manage Own Performance in a Business Environment | |
| 2 | Improve Own Performance in a Business Environment | |
| 3 | Work in a Business Environment | |
| 4 | Communicate in a Business Environment | Information selected, information formatted, minutes of meetings, feedback received |
| 6 | Work with Other People in a Business Environment | Minutes, emails, performance reviews |
| 8 | Produce Documents in a Business Environment | Documents produced |
| 24 | Make and Receive Telephone Calls | Telephone logs, memos, emails, messages |
| 25 | Use Electronic Message Systems | Messages |
| 26 | Use Diary Systems | Diary, letters, emails, memos |
| 31 | Provide Reception Services | |
| 34 | Deliver, Monitor and Evaluate Customer Service to External Customers | Feedback received |
| 36 | Research Information | Notes of informal meetings, records |
| 37 | Store and Retrieve Information | Information |
| 38 | Archive Information | Memos, information, records |
| 43 | Use Office Equipment | |
| 52 | Use Occupational and Safety Guidelines when using Keyboards | |

**Now that you have completed your Induction, you will need to get ready for your next assessor visit. This section focuses on your performance in your role and how this can be improved.**

**In this section you will find a range of activities to help you prepare and gather evidence for your assessment related to the following topics:**

1. **Preparing to work**
2. **Working in Business and improving own performance**

Topic areas that may be discussed include:

- Your role at work
- Setting targets and goals
- Responsibilities at work
- Setting standards
- Being organised and meeting deadlines
- Identifying key aspects of your employment

During your next visit, your assessor will want to observe you in the workplace carrying out activities that show your ability to do your job and showing that you have a good knowledge and understanding of your organisation. It is worth remembering that this observation needs to be of real-life activities. Simulated activities are not permitted.

Your assessor may wish to talk with your line manager/supervisor about your progress through the Apprenticeship programme and to make sure you are on track to complete it in a reasonable amount of time. It would be a good idea to let your manager know in advance when the assessor may want to see them.

For this visit, it would be useful if you could gather certain pieces of evidence. For example, how you set goals and targets you have to follow at work and any action plans you put in place to make sure these goals and targets are met.

2

# 1. PREPARING TO WORK

When you first begin working, it can sometimes be quite difficult to understand all the different forms and ways of working. This may well be the first time that you have entered the world of work. The first few weeks can be challenging, especially as you are new to the organisation, you don't know anyone and you are trying to find your way around.

Working in business administration, you are often the first point of contact for many staff when they have a question, so it is important that you learn about the organisation very quickly.

## KNOWLEDGE AND UNDERSTANDING

To make sure that you have a good understanding of how your organisation operates, the following activities look at how you fit into your organisation. You will look at your organisation's policies and procedures and any laws that may affect your work. As your role demands that you are organised and work to keep high standards at all times, in Task 2 you will create a 'to do' list to plan your activities for the day.

It is important that you are aware of the sector in which your organisation operates and how your role adds value to this. You will also look at any issues concerning your organisation, such as environmental issues, and look at how the public may view the organisation you work for. You also need to think about your career path and identify any possible opportunities that may be open to you, either within your current organisation or outside it. Finally, you will identify key aspects of your employment, in particular your payslip, to make sure that you understand the information on your payslip when you receive this from your employer.

The following activities will help you to demonstrate your understanding of your current role and the part you play in your organisation.

**BTEC** Unit 1: 1.2, 1.5, 2.1
**NVQ** Unit 1: 1.1, 3.8; Unit 3: 6.4; Unit 6: 1.7, 1.8, 7.1
**WorkSkills** Unit 2: 1.3, 1.4, 2.3

### Task 1

While at work, there are rules that need to be followed. The organisation you work for sets these rules out in the form of policies and procedures.

In this task, you are going to find key documents your organisation holds concerning your employment and what to do about any problems you may have while you are at work. You need to find a copy of your organisation's:

- grievance procedure
- Code of Conduct.

1. Are there any other policies/procedures which you think are necessary for you to carry out your role, such as flex-time rules, holidays, etc? Make a note of these policies and procedures in the space provided below.

2. How do you think legislation supports employees in the workplace?

3. If you needed to make a grievance, what would you do?

4. Describe the responsibilities employers have in the workplace.

2

**BTEC** Unit 1: 5.1, 5.2
**NVQ** Unit 1: 1.5, 1.8, 1.9, 2.1, 2.2, 3.1, 3.2, 3.4, 3.5, 3.6, 3.7, 4.1

## Task 2

In your role as an administrator, it is vital that you are organised and that you are able to prioritise tasks so that work is completed by the deadlines set, and to the correct standard.

1. In this task, you are going to plan your typical work day and write a 'to do' list to make sure that you are organised throughout the day.

   Make sure your list includes everything you are planning to do, including coffee and lunch breaks. Prioritise the tasks and give them a deadline so you can easily see which are the most important. The first line of the table below has been completed for you as an example.

| Task(s) to be completed | What I have to do to get this task done? | How long will it take me? | How important is this task? | Priority number |
|---|---|---|---|---|
| Open post and distribute to department | • Make sure post is in the correct place<br>• All post distributed to the correct recipients | 20 minutes | High | 1 |
| | | | | |
| | | | | |
| | | | | |
| | | | | |
| | | | | |

Why do you need to sort and distribute the post as soon as possible?

2. In the space below, answer the following questions.

| Question | Your answer |
|---|---|
| Why is it important to be organised? | |
| Why should you continually try to set high standards in your work? How do you set these standards? | |
| What would you do if you realised you couldn't meet a deadline for a task you had been asked to complete? | |
| Who do you speak to when you realise there is a problem with completing a task on time? | |
| Describe the type of problems that you come across in your role. | |
| When problems occur in your role, who do you keep informed of progress to resolve these problems? | |

2

**NVQ** Unit 6: 1.1, 1.2, 1.3, 1.4, 1.5, 1.6
**WorkSkills** Unit 2: 3.1, 3.2, 3.3, 3.4, 3.5

## Task 3

In this set of activities, you are going to take a closer look at the sector in which your organisation operates. You will also think about what you do in your organisation, that is, what your actual role is and how you fit into your organisational structure. Finally there is an activity looking at issues in your sector and how these issues are viewed by the public. This will help to give you a good overview of the business you are in and help you to contribute positively to the overall aims and objectives of your organisation.

1. In the space below, answer the following questions. You may need help from a line manager or colleague to answer some of them.

| | Question | Your answer |
|---|---|---|
| 1. | Describe the sector in which your organisation operates. | |
| 2. | What is your organisation's mission and purpose? | |
| 3. | Thinking of the sector that your organisation is operating in, how does your organisation compare with other organisations in other sectors? For example, if you are working in the education sector, how would this be different if you were in a manufacturing organisation? | |

2. In the space below, describe your role and then on a separate piece of paper draw a chart to show how your role fits into your organisation's structure.

   a. Describe your role. What are your responsibilities? What are you expected to do?

   b. How does your role contribute to the daily operation of the organisation? For example, if you are working on reception, do you greet visitors and make sure they are directed to the correct place/person?

3. In this activity, you are going to think about how the general public view your organisation and the sector it operates in, concentrating particularly on an area of public concern. For example, if you work in the education sector, do some people think that adults paying a fee for their course do not get value for money? Or, if you work in the manufacturing sector, has there been concern about pollution?

Issues will vary from sector to sector. The table below should help you think about your sector and any public concerns that exist. You can continue on a separate piece of paper, if necessary

| What sector do you work in? | Outline an area of public concern which is relevant to the sector in which you work. | Describe how these issues of public concern have affected public views of the sector, that is, has anything happened which may influence these views, has the industry put in place some new safety mechanisms, etc. |
|---|---|---|
| | | |

**BTEC** Unit 1: 6.3
**NVQ** Unit 2: 1.4, 1.5
**WorkSkills** Unit 1: 3.1, 3.2; Unit 2: 4.1, 4.2, 4.3

## Task 4

In the following activities you are going to begin the process of looking at your career path, and opportunities you may want to take as your career progresses. You will also think about the information you will need to make sure that, if you want to continue with study or other professional development, you can act quickly when the time arrives.

1. It may be that you do not wish to continue on to do a Level 3 Apprenticeship, but prefer to take opportunities available to you in your organisation. If there are other opportunities that could be available to you, list them in the table below. Complete the sections in the table below; the first line has been completed for you as an example.

| What are the career pathways available in your sector? | What are the career pathways available in your organisation? | What sources of information do you need to make sure you choose the correct pathway? |
|---|---|---|
| Continue to Level 3 Apprenticeship in Business Administration | Promotion from Admin Assistant to Business Administrator | • Specification for L3<br>• Information on how long it will take to complete L3 |
| | | |
| | | |
| | | |
| | | |

2. In the space below, write a short paragraph identifying what your next steps are going to be in your intended career pathway. For example, do you need to speak to someone in your organisation, or do you need to speak to your assessor?

**WorkSkills** Unit 8: 2.1, 2.2, 2.4

## Task 5

This task asks you to take a closer look at your payslip and the terms and conditions of your employment. It also asks you to think about information that you need to keep up to date with your employer.

1. Your payslip.

   a. On page 22 is an example of a payslip. Yours may look very similar. Look at the image: it has a series of numbers and arrows pointing to various parts of the payslip. For each of the numbers identified on the payslip, complete the related area in the table on page 22 with a brief description of what each part of the payslip means. The first line in the table has been completed for you.

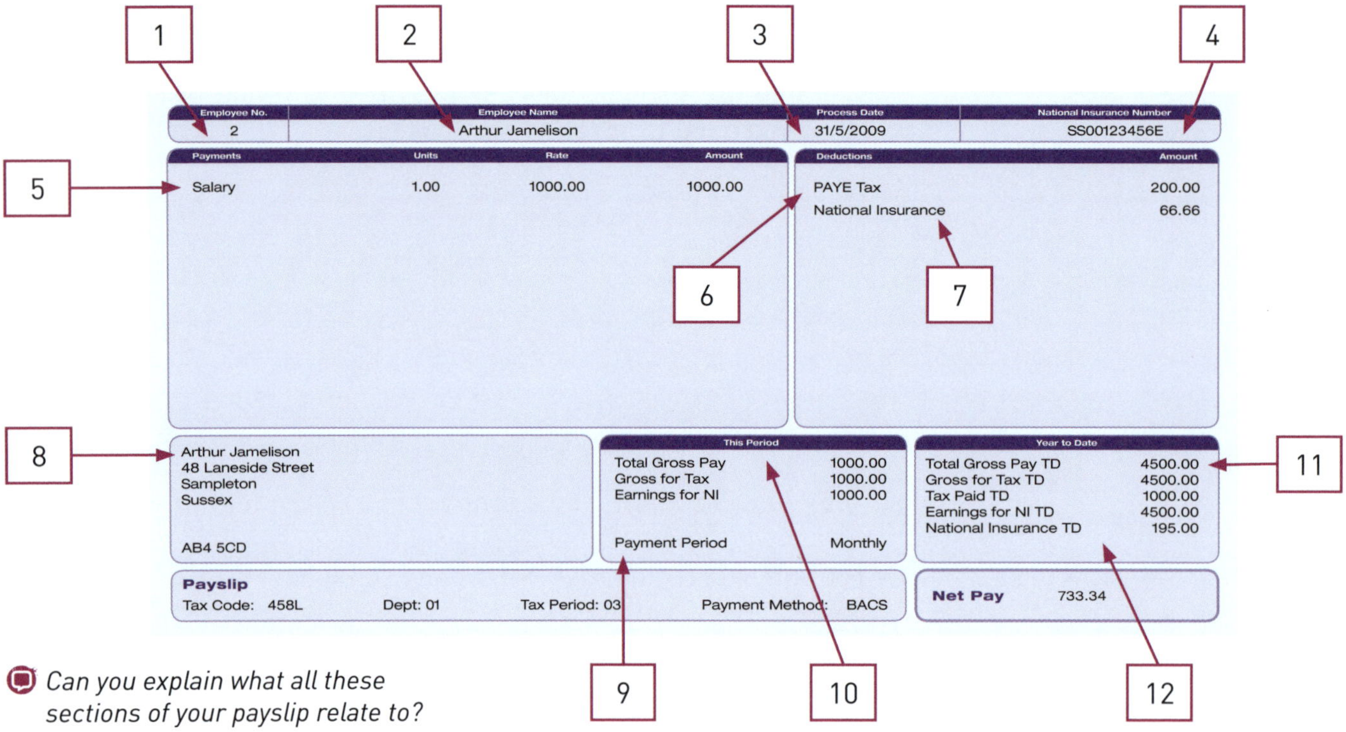


*Can you explain what all these sections of your payslip relate to?*

| No. | Item | Description |
|---|---|---|
| 1. | Employee no. | Each employee in an organisation is given a unique number that they keep throughout their employment. This number means that an employee's records can be found easily on the pay system. |
| 2. | | |
| 3. | | |
| 4. | | |
| 5. | | |
| 6. | | |
| 7. | | |
| 8. | | |
| 9. | | |
| 10. | | |
| 11. | | |
| 12. | | |

b. In the space below, note any differences on your payslip, compared to the sample one opposite.

2. You will have been given a contract of employment when you began your Apprenticeship with your organisation. In this task, you will explain the main terms and conditions of your contract given in the table below.

| Main terms and conditions | What is on your contract? |
|---|---|
| The name of your employer | |
| Your place of work | |
| Your job title | |
| The date on which your employment began | |
| Your hours of work | |
| Your pay and any other associated benefits, e.g. sick pay, holiday pay | |
| Period of notice if you or your employer wish to terminate the contract | |

2

## EVIDENCE GATHERING

In this activity you will identify an area of your work that will show evidence of how you operate as an administrator. *Your assessor will help you to identify suitable items of evidence.*

You need to gather evidence of activity in areas of your work to demonstrate:

**BTEC** Unit 1: 5.1, 5.2
**NVQ** Unit 1: 1.8, 1.9, 2.1, 2.2, 3.1, 3.2, 3.4, 3.5, 3.6, 3.7, 3.8, 4.1; Unit 6: 2.4, 8.6; Unit 26: 2.2, 2.3, 2.4, 2.5

How you carry out your daily duties in a typical day.

Suggested evidence may include:

- completed 'to do' list/daily plan
- witness testimony from your line manager describing how you carry out particular activities
- organisational procedures.

**BTEC** Unit 1: 5.3
**NVQ** Unit 1: 1.2, 1.3, 1.4, 1.6, 1.7, 1.10; Unit 3: 1.4, 6.4; Unit 6: 7.1, 7.2, 7.4

## PROFESSIONAL DISCUSSION

Your assessor will carry out a professional discussion with you that will capture the evidence needed to prove your level of knowledge and understanding of topic areas.

Below are some topic areas you will need to think about when preparing for the professional discussion with your assessor:

- Organisational procedures, including legal requirements in relation to discrimination legislation
- Setting realistic targets at work to make sure planned deadlines are met
- Communication with colleagues about changing plans and keeping people informed
- How you can learn from mistakes and how you can learn from other colleagues
- Applying organisational values and who to speak to if you have questions

*Your assessor will plan the content of your professional discussion and will advise you to help you to prepare beforehand. The professional discussion may cover more than this section of your Workbook.*

## Discussion process

The discussion process offers you the chance to show your knowledge of the sector in which you are currently working and how you can make sure that your contribution to the organisation makes a difference. The discussion shows your assessor how you plan your time, set yourself targets to make sure tasks are completed on time and also that you know who you should speak to when there are problems. This process will also look at organisational procedures in your company and how these are applied across the workforce.

To prepare for your professional discussion, you should think about how you could answer questions such as the following:

- What is the importance of following organisational procedures?
- Why must you be aware of discrimination legislation in the workplace?
- How do you make sure your time is planned so that you can achieve the tasks set by others?
- How do you agree realistic targets?
- How do you keep colleagues informed of your progress through tasks and why do you think this is important, especially when plans change?
- In what different ways do you keep your colleagues informed of your progress?
- How do you get assistance when problems occur at work?
- What are the benefits of learning from your mistakes?
- How do you try to learn from others at work?
- How do you make sure you represent the values of the organisation in your work?
- Who do you ask if you have questions about organisational policies and procedures?

2

# 2. WORKING IN BUSINESS AND IMPROVING OWN PERFORMANCE

It is important that while you are at work, you always seek ways of improving your performance. This can happen in many different ways, including taking on new challenges, learning new skills, taking on new study opportunities. Identifying ways to improve processes and procedures in your current role can improve your own performance, as well as that of the organisation. It is important to realise that you can make some improvements yourself. Recognising what these improvements could be is the first step towards a fulfilling career.

*There are lots of courses available that can help you progress in your career.*

**NVQ** Unit 1: 4.2, 4.3; Unit 2: 1.4, 1.5, 3.1, 3.2
**WorkSkills** Unit 9: 1.1
**PLTS** SM1, SM6
**BTEC** Unit 1: 4.2

## KNOWLEDGE AND UNDERSTANDING

In this section, you will look at ways in which you can improve your own performance at work. By carrying out a skills audit, you will be able to see the skills you currently have, and where there are gaps. Career progression is an important part of your future plans. You will think about where you see yourself in the future, and identify any development opportunities you think you need in order to get to your desired goal. Feedback is vital if you are to improve your performance, and Task 2 looks at gathering feedback on your performance from a variety of sources in your organisation. To pull all the above together, you will produce a learning plan, and finally you will look at how you are going to approach new challenges in your career.

### Task 1

As you are currently undertaking an Apprenticeship in Business & Administration, there may be a clear progression route within your organisation that will allow you to work towards promotion at key times during your career there. However, Business & Administration equips you with many varied and useful skills that can be transferred into other areas and can take you in many different directions.

In this activity, you are going to think about the skills you currently have. You will carry out a skills audit to find your starting point, and then look at different progression routes in your chosen career. You also need to think about the possible next steps in your career, once you have completed your Level 2 Apprenticeship, and the skills you need to achieve this progression.

1. Skills audit

In this activity, you are going to look at your current skills and rate them on a scale from 1 to 5 (1 being strong, 5 being weak). You are also going to look at the knowledge and skills you will need in the future.

| Knowledge and skills that are important for my current role | My ability rating 1–5 (or strong/ weak/somewhere in between) | How am I going to address these weaknesses? (e.g. further study, professional development) |
|---|---|---|
| | | |

| Knowledge and skills important for my *future* career | My ability rating 1–5 (or strong/ weak/somewhere in between) | How am I going to address these weaknesses? (e.g. further study, professional development) |
|---|---|---|
| | | |

2. Career progression

Think about the options for you to progress your career. For example, as a Level 2 Apprentice, your job role is probably trainee administration assistant or office assistant. What is the next step up for you, either within your organisation, or in a different organisation? Write your answer in the space below.

3. Development opportunities

Thinking about where you want to go after completing this apprenticeship, what development opportunities are open to you? These can either be within your organisation, or in your local college, community, etc.

**NVQ** Unit 2: 2.1, 2.2, 2.3; Unit 3: 6.3
**WorkSkills** Unit 9: 2.4, 2.5
**PLTS** RL: 1, 3, 4, 5
SM: 2

## Task 2

Getting feedback on your performance at work is crucial to your development. Feedback can come from a variety of sources:

- customers – both internal and external
- your assessor – through your action plan
- your line manager – through appraisals or informal feedback on completion of tasks
- colleagues.

The key is to use feedback to your advantage and to learn from it.

Feedback can really help you to move forward in your role.

In this task, you are going to collect various forms of feedback from as many of the people you deal with on a daily basis as possible. Collect this feedback, and record it in a table, such as that given below. From this feedback you can then produce your own action plan to help improve your performance at work.

1. You can use the templates below and on page 30 to record your feedback and produce your action plan, or you could draw up your own. The first line of the feedback form has been completed for you as an example.

| Date of feedback | Who was the feedback from? | Details of the feedback | How am I going to use this feedback | Do I need any further learning/development? |
|---|---|---|---|---|
| 27.10.10 | Sales Manager | He was pleased with the high standard of my work, which meant that the document went out to the customer on time | Make sure that these high standards I have set at work are maintained and improved | Further IT training, particularly in Excel to allow me to work on more detailed spreadsheets |
| | | | | |
| | | | | |
| | | | | |

2

2. You are now going to produce an action plan, based on your findings from the feedback you received from colleagues and customers. This will form the basis for your learning plan. The first line has been completed for you as an example.

| Action | What information do I need? | What will the outcome be? | Date to be completed by |
|---|---|---|---|
| Undertake an intermediate Excel course | • Details of local courses<br>• Contact college, local community centres<br>• Speak to Line Manager re training on Excel | I will be able to complete more complicated spreadsheets, therefore making a greater contribution to the sales department | December 2010 |
| | | | |
| | | | |

**BTEC** Unit 1: 6.2
**NVQ** Unit 2: 3.2, 3.3, 3.4
**WorkSkills** Unit 9: 1.4, 1.5, 1.6, 2.1, 2.2
**PLTS** SM: 2, 3, 5, 7
RL: 1, 2, 3

## Task 3

In this task, you are going to create a learning plan to follow. This plan can be based on the feedback you collected in the previous task, gaps in your skills audit, or other learning you have identified that you will need to take you further in your career.

You will already have been given an action plan by your assessor which will allow you to complete your Apprenticeship in a timely manner. The learning plan that you create now should work alongside this earlier action plan. You should also discuss this with your assessor the next time you meet.

1. To complete this task, you need to:
   - complete a learning plan similar to that opposite, and
   - think about where your previous learning has been successful and include any reflections or comments you have on this learning.

   The first line of the second table has been completed for you as an example.

   You may use the templates opposite if you wish; however, if you would like to create your own templates, then you are free to do so. If you do create your own templates, make sure that all key learning and key dates are included on it and allow a space for comments and reflections once you have completed the learning.

| Learning plan | |
|---|---|
| Name: | Organisation: |
| Job role/Title: | Department: |
| Date created: | Date for review: |

| Skills and knowledge requiring action | Activity to support this | Achieved by | Review date |
|---|---|---|---|
| | | | |
| **Area for development** | **Activity to support this** | **Achieved by** | **Review date** |
| | | | |
| **Reflection**<br>Use this space to add any notes on learning undertaken, if anything has happened as a result of this additional activity and if anything has occurred which has meant that you may not be able to complete by the due date, e.g. personal circumstances | | | |

| Previous learning I have undertaken | What did I do that made it successful? | Comments/reflections |
|---|---|---|
| GCSE Business Studies | I made lots of notes and tried to think of real-life examples which related to the topics we studied | This helped me remember the main topics and I was able to understand the theory better |
| | | |
| | | |
| | | |
| | | |

2

Where your previous learning has been successful, have you told anyone about this; for example, a teacher, or a friend or colleague? Add some comments about this here.

**BTEC** Unit 1: 4.2
**NVQ** Unit 1: 2.3, 2.4, 4.2, 4.3

## Task 4

As a result of looking forward and being pro-active about your career, you may well be faced with new challenges at work. How will you react to these new challenges?

Answer the following questions in the spaces provided.

1. What are the benefits for you and your organisation of taking on new challenges?

2. Why would you agree to take on new challenges if they came up?

3. Once you have taken on new challenges, how do you adapt to a new way of working?

## EVIDENCE GATHERING

In this activity you will identify an area of your work that will show evidence of how you operate at work. *Your assessor will help you to identify suitable items of evidence.*

You need to gather evidence of activity in areas of your work to demonstrate:

**NVQ** Unit 1: 4.2, 4.3; Unit 2: 1.4, 1.5, 3.1, 3.2
**WorkSkills** Unit 2: 4.1, 4.2; Unit 9: 1.1, 2.3
**PLTS** SM: 1, 6
RL: 4
**BTEC** Unit 1: 6.3

a. How you have assessed your skills and learning requirements.

Suggested evidence may include:

- skills audit showing your current skills and how you plan to address the weaknesses
- career progression chart.

**NVQ** Unit 2: 2.1, 2.2, 2.3; Unit 3: 6.3
**WorkSkills** Unit 9: 2.3

b. That you have received feedback from colleagues, customers, your line manager, etc., and used this feedback to form an action plan to address any issues.

Suggested evidence may include:

- table showing collection of informal feedback from colleagues
- appraisal form completed by line manager
- action plan to address issues
- copy of action plan set out by assessor
- witness testimony.

**NVQ** Unit 2: 3.1, 3.2
**WorkSkills** Unit 9: 1.1, 2.3
**PLTS** SM: 2, 3
RL: 1, 2, 3

c. You have created a learning plan as a result of collecting feedback, created a skills audit from any other data collected, and also reflected on previous learning.

Suggested evidence may include:

- learning plan complete with dates for completion of activities and review dates to identify where learning has or has not taken place
- reflections on previous learning.

**BTEC** Unit 1: 4.2, 6.1
**NVQ** Unit 1: 2.4; Unit 2: 1.1, 1.2, 1.3
**WorkSkills** Unit 9: 1.2, 1.3

## PROFESSIONAL DISCUSSION

Your assessor will carry out a professional discussion with you, which will capture the evidence needed to prove your level of knowledge and understanding of topic areas.

Below are some topic areas you will need to think about when preparing for the professional discussion with your assessor:

- The purpose of always improving performance at work and understanding how personal development can improve your own work and that of others
- Accepting feedback from others

- Taking on new challenges and adapting to change
- The benefits of completing learning on time
- The disadvantages of learning not being completed on time

*Your assessor will plan the content of your professional discussion and will advise you to help you to prepare beforehand. The professional discussion may cover more than this section of your Workbook.*

## Discussion process

The discussion process offers you the chance to show that you are always looking at ways to improve your own performance. A career in business administration can offer wide and varied opportunities. If you are an ambitious person, then being able to adapt to change and improve your own career prospects will help you gain the relevant skills and qualifications to take you forward.

To prepare for your professional discussion, you should think about how you could answer questions such as the following:

- Why do you think it is important to always try to improve your performance at work?
- How would you encourage feedback from others in your organisation?
- Why is it important to accept new challenges at work?
- How do you adapt to change in an organisation?
- What do you think the risks are of not completing a learning programme on time?
- What are the benefits of completing learning on time?

# 3

**Now that you have completed your induction and preparation for work visits and assessments, you will need to begin to prepare for your next assessor visit. The following pages will guide you through the steps you need to take.**

**In this section you will find a range of activities to help you prepare and gather evidence for your assessment related to the following topics:**

1. Undertaking administrative functions effectively
2. Using technology in the workplace
3. Preparing business documents
4. Carrying out research effectively
5. Archiving and storage

This will be the third visit your assessor will make. Now that you have settled into your Apprenticeship, and are working to collect evidence, your assessor will observe you in the workplace completing some of the activities you carry out on a day-to-day basis. Photographs or video are acceptable forms of evidence and may be used in your portfolio. Remember, you may need to get permission from your employer before photographs or recordings are taken.

Your assessor may also wish to meet your line manager or supervisor during the visit. This meeting will help your manager understand the type of work you need to do to collect the evidence needed for your portfolio.

3

# 1. UNDERTAKING ADMINISTRATIVE FUNCTIONS EFFECTIVELY

This sequence of activities will help you demonstrate your knowledge and understanding of administrative functions in an office environment. Working in an office requires a variety of tasks to be undertaken. Your role will present challenges, and at times you will need to prioritise and make decisions about which tasks are most important.

These activities will help you to explore some of the day-to-day functions that take place in an office, and will help you to undertake them confidently.

## KNOWLEDGE AND UNDERSTANDING

Through the tasks in this section you will demonstrate your understanding of specific administrative functions within an office environment. You will be able to identify the importance of keeping documents up to date. You will also be able to identify when and what to prioritise so tasks are completed by the deadline, while maintaining confidentiality and security.

An important feature of your role is recording information accurately. In this section, you will gain a thorough understanding of the need to make sure accuracy is maintained at all times, even while working to tight deadlines.

**BTEC** Unit 2: 7.2
**NVQ** Unit 26: 1.2, 1.3, 2.1

### Task 1

In your role as an administrator, keeping a diary is an important task. There are generally two different types of diaries that can be used in an office – manual and electronic. In the table opposite you need to identify the different types of diaries in each of these categories, explain how they are used and describe the information you think will be placed in these diaries.

It is worth remembering that in each type of diary there are different forms of diary. For example, in 'manual', you may like to think about the traditional desk diary, as well as the wall chart planner.

Remember also to think about confidentiality and security issues in your findings.

| Type of diary | Features | How and where the type of diary is used | Information needed to keep diary |
|---|---|---|---|
| Manual | | | |
| Electronic | | | |

**BTEC** Unit 2: 1.1, 2.1, 2.2, 2.3

## Task 2

It is worth remembering that communication with either internal or external people in an office often means that an action has to be carried out. This could be, for example:

- a change of diary appointment
- a change to work plans
- sending out mail.

Before you begin this task, find a copy of the following documents:

- the company policy/procedure for answering telephone calls
- information on other phone systems
- the company policy on dealing with mail (post).

You should also visit the Royal Mail website to find the following information:

- different types of envelope sizes
- the cost of postage
- how to deal with parcels
- how to send a parcel or letter which needs to be tracked.

You should also visit appropriate websites to find different telephone systems that are currently on the market and which could be used by an organisation.

Communication in an office occurs in many different ways. In this activity, you will produce a PowerPoint presentation (5–10 minutes maximum), which you will deliver to your colleagues and assessor. This presentation will focus on communication in relation to office telephone systems and mail services.

The presentation must:

- examine the telephone system used in your organisation and explain its features and how it helps your daily activities

- discuss other telephone systems and their uses
- explain how internal and external mail is dealt with in your organisation and why it is important to deal with mail quickly and efficiently
- explain how postage is calculated and the types of packages that your organisation sends.

*What needs to be done to organise a meeting?*

BTEC Unit 2: 5.1, 5.2, 5.3

## Task 3

Your line manager/supervisor has asked you to arrange a staff meeting for the whole team to attend.

The meeting is to take place on Monday morning at 9.30am and all staff in the team must attend. You are aware that Monday mornings are the busiest times for booking meeting rooms and you may need to negotiate with some colleagues to book a room.

1. In the space below, describe what you would do to make sure this meeting was organised correctly and how you would communicate with your team members to make sure they were fully up to date with arrangements.

2. A team meeting is just one type of meeting that can take place in an organisation. In the space below there are some other examples of meetings. You need to:
   - identify the purpose of the meetings already listed for you
   - then list as many different types of meetings as you can
   - identify the purpose of these other types of meetings.

   You may continue on another page if you wish. The first line has been completed for you as an example.

| **Type of meeting** | **Purpose** |
|---|---|
| Team meeting | • *To allow line manager/supervisor to pass information to all team members*<br>• *To allow team members to update on tasks being undertaken* |
| Board meeting | |
| Committee meeting | |
| | |
| | |
| | |

3. Finally, write a short step-by-step guide on to how to organise a meeting. You need to focus on the information needed to make sure the meeting is organised correctly and where you need to go to get that information.

continued

3

BTEC Unit: 2: 6.1, 6.2, 6.3
NVQ Unit 26: 3.5, 3.6

## Task 4

As an administrator, you may be faced with arranging travel and accommodation for your line manager or other members of staff in your team. Planning and organising travel is an important task and you must check that all aspects of the travel planned are covered to make sure no problems occur. Very often, you will have to work to a budget and to company procedures/guidelines when organising travel.

Before you carry out this task, find a copy of the following document:

- company policy/procedure/guidelines on travel.

1. Read the following scenario. Use the space opposite to explain what procedures you would go through to make these arrangements, and who you would need to contact to make sure arrangements were finalised.

*Your line manager has asked you to make arrangements for her to travel to Paris for a company training course. The training course is being held in the Radisson Blu (SAS) Hotel in the centre of Paris, starting on 30 November and ending on 2 December. She wants to stay the night before the training course in the same hotel and wishes to travel from her local airport. She would like to fly to Paris as late as possible and will leave her car at the UK airport. She will travel back immediately after the end of the course, which is due to finish at approximately 2.30pm on the final afternoon.*

2. In the space below, describe the types of problems you may encounter, or have met, when organising travel.

## EVIDENCE GATHERING

In this activity you will identify an area of your work that will capture evidence of how you operate as an administrator. *Your assessor will help you to identify suitable items of evidence.*

You need to gather evidence of activity in areas of your work to demonstrate:

**BTEC** Unit 2: 7.1, 7.2; Unit 3: 1.1, 1.2
**NVQ** Unit 6: 6.2; Unit 26: 1.3, 2.1, 3.2, 3.3, 3.4, 3.5, 3.6, 3.7

How you have maintained a diary on a day-to-day basis.

Suggested evidence may include:

- a copy of an appropriate diary covering approximately one month of entries
- a written log of any diary changes you make, their impact on other members of the team and how you handled these changes
- a short report on how you manage a diary in your organisation, including how you deal with prioritising requests.

3

**BTEC** Unit 2: 7.1, 7.2
**NVQ** Unit 26: 2.4, 2.5, 2.6, 2.7, 2.8, 3.2, 3.4, 3.7

## PUTTING IT INTO PRACTICE

This activity will help your assessor to examine your competence by observing you carrying out workplace activities. This might include asking related questions to test your underpinning knowledge.

Making changes to a diary.

During this observation, your assessor will want to see that you can access the diary system correctly, make necessary changes, communicate these changes and store the information securely. Your assessor may also wish to ask you about the advantages and disadvantages of the system you are using.

**BTEC** Unit 2: 2.1, 6.1, 6.3, 7.1
**NVQ** Unit 26: 1.1, 1.2, 1.3, 2.2, 2.3, 2.4, 2.5, 2.6, 2.7, 2.8, 3.3, 3.7

## PROFESSIONAL DISCUSSION

Your assessor will carry out a professional discussion with you, to capture the evidence needed to prove your level of knowledge and understanding of topic areas.

Below are some topic areas you will need to think about when preparing for the professional discussion with your assessor:

- Diary systems
- Dealing with changes and ensuring systems are kept up to date
- Planning and organisation skills
- Communication with members of your team
- Managing deadlines and prioritising work

*Your assessor will plan the content of your professional discussion and will advise you to help you to prepare beforehand. The professional discussion may cover more than this section of your Workbook.*

### Discussion process

The discussion process offers you the chance to show that you have a working knowledge in your role as an administrator. These questions will also enable you to demonstrate your understanding of some of the key issues you need to think about when you are working in an office environment.

To prepare for your professional discussion, you should think about how you could answer questions such as the following:

- How do you deal with information that needs to be kept securely?
- How do you prioritise your work to make sure that all deadlines are met and work is completed on time?
- How do you communicate changes in plans to other members of your team/organisation?
- What is the purpose of keeping a diary system?

3

- Why is it important to make sure that all travel/accommodation arrangements are accurate and thoroughly checked?
- In your role, how do you deal with changes to plans while at the same time ensuring all deadlines are met?

# 2. USING TECHNOLOGY IN THE WORKPLACE

In this section, you will carry out a series of activities that will help you to use the technology currently available in your workplace effectively and efficiently. In your administrative role, the more common types of machinery you will use include a computer, photocopier, fax machine, scanner, mailroom equipment, and so on. In recent years, the use of computers has transformed how the workplace operates and has greatly affected the role of the administrator.

When your assessor visits, they will want to watch you using different pieces of equipment in your working environment to make sure that you are able to use each type of equipment for the purpose for which it is meant.

## KNOWLEDGE AND UNDERSTANDING

The following activities take you through a series of steps in using office machinery and technology. The activities will show your knowledge of using different types of machines, as well as your ability to identify problems with the machinery, and to deal with them according to the manufacturer's guidelines.

You will also look at the impact information technology has had in the workplace, especially email and the internet, and how this is used in everyday working life. Communication is a key role of an administrator, so accuracy and keeping email systems up to date is crucial to make sure messages are responded to in a timely manner.

*It's important that you know how to use all office equipment properly.*

**BTEC** Unit 2: 3.1
**NVQ** Unit 43: 1.1, 4.1, 7.1, 7.5

## Task 1

In the table below, list all the different types of equipment you use in your workplace on a daily basis and state the purpose/task for which you use them. This table will look very similar to a log, or diary of when and how you use equipment. Over the period of a week, you should update your table every time you use a different piece of equipment. You should also state any problems you had using this equipment and how you resolved these problems.

The table headings used below are only suggestions. You could use your own if you wish. The first line has been completed for you.

| Date | Purpose/Task | Equipment used | Problems met/resolved |
|---|---|---|---|
| 3.9.10 | Photocopying agenda for team meeting | Photocopier | Paper jam – I had to lift the lid of the photocopier and remove paper which was jammed in the rollers |
| | | | |
| | | | |
| | | | |
| | | | |

Continue on a new page if you need to.

**BTEC** Unit 2: 3.2
**NVQ** Unit 43: 4.2, 7.2

## Task 2

For each of the pieces of equipment you have listed in Task 1, find a copy of the manufacturer's instructions, the organisational procedures for using these pieces of equipment and any other written instructions that have been produced in your workplace for operating the equipment.

1. Make notes in the table below, saying where these instructions and procedures can be found.

| Equipment | Location of manufacturer's instructions | Location of organisational procedures | Other instructions or notes |
|---|---|---|---|
| | | | |
| | | | |
| | | | |
| | | | |
| | | | |
| | | | |
| | | | |
| | | | |
| | | | |

2. Give a brief explanation below of why it is important to follow manufacturers' instructions when using office equipment, especially when you have any problems with this equipment. Refer back to the table in Task 1 to remind yourself of any problems you had.

**BTEC** Unit 3: 1.1, 1.2
**NVQ** Unit 25: 1.1, 1.2

## Task 3

1. In the table below, show the different types of current IT that may be used in the workplace. You will also need to state the benefits of using this technology in a business environment. Don't forget to include software and any other devices that you use regularly.

The first line has been completed for you as an example.

| IT type | Purpose | Benefits of using this |
|---|---|---|
| Email | To send messages electronically to email addresses on contact list | • Can be accessed in some cases 24/7<br>• Allows exchange of information between people<br>• Allows people to be copied into different messages<br>• Attachments can be sent |
| | | |
| | | |
| | | |
| | | |

| IT type | Purpose | Benefits of using this |
|---|---|---|
| | | |
| | | |

2. In the table below, you are going to look at electronic messaging systems. You will think about what they are, and describe how they are used. The first line has been completed for you as an example.

| Electronic message system | Description of how it is used |
|---|---|
| Text message (SMS) | Used to send short messages to friends and other people who own a mobile phone. Can also be sent to work colleagues to remind them of meetings, etc. |
| | |
| | |

**NVQ** Unit 25: 1.1, 1.2, 1.3, 1.4, 1.5

## Task 4

Produce a PowerPoint presentation about using email in a business environment for delivery to your assessor and other apprentices or people you work with.

Your presentation should look at:

- the features of different email systems
- how to send emails
- why it is important to keep an email system up to date
- how to delete emails from the system
- why you need to use clear language when writing emails.

You might also like to include a 'dos' and 'don'ts' section in your presentation that focuses on good practice when writing emails.

**NVQ** Unit 4: 2.2; Unit 25: 2.4; Unit 43: 6.1, 7.4

## Task 5

Explain what you would do in the following situations.

| Situation | Your explanation – what should you do? |
|---|---|
| You have received an email that needs a response by the end of the day. You are unsure if you can get all the information ready by that deadline. | |
| Your boss has asked you to file all emails that are more than a month old in a series of folders. Why should you do this? | |
| You have accidently sent an email to John Smith in Accounts instead of John Smith in Technical Support. What should you do? | |
| Your friend has sent you an email that you find quite funny, but it involves some office gossip. What should you do with this email? | |
| You have just completed a job on the photocopier. How should you leave the machine once you are finished? | |

3

## EVIDENCE GATHERING

In this activity you will identify an area of your work that will capture evidence of how you operate as an administrator. *Your assessor will help you to identify suitable items of evidence.*

You will need to gather evidence of activity in areas of your work to demonstrate:

**NVQ** Unit 4: 6.1, 6.2, 6.3. 6.4, 6.5, 6.8; Unit 8: 5.3, 5.6, 5.7, 5.9; Unit 25: 2.1, 2.2, 2.4, 2.5, 2.6

Sending and receiving emails, using IT safely and securely, keeping an email system up to date.

Suggested evidence may include:

- witness statements
- copies of emails sent and received (permission may be needed first)
- screen prints of folders
- screen prints showing items to be deleted
- PowerPoint presentation created by you.

**NVQ** Unit 4: 1.1, 1.2, 5.2, 6.1, 6.8; Unit 25: 1.1, 1.2, 1.3, 1.4, 1.5, 2.1, 2.2, 2.3, 2.4, 2.5, 2.6; Unit 43: 1.1, 1.2, 1.3, 4.1, 7.1, 7.9; Unit 52: 2.1, 2.2, 2.3, 2.4 **BTEC** Unit 2: 1.2

## PUTTING IT INTO PRACTICE

This activity will help your assessor to examine your competence by watching you carry out workplace activities. This might include asking related questions to test your underpinning knowledge.

Using an email system securely and safely.

**WorkSkills** Unit 7: 1.2, 2.2, 2.5; Unit 9: 1.6, 1.4 **PLTS** IE: 2, 4, 5, 6 SM: 2, 3, 5

The assessor will want to see that you deal competently with incoming and outgoing emails, including keeping the system up to date, deleting emails when necessary, filing emails and responding to emails in a timely manner, using appropriate language. Because of confidentiality issues, you may need to gain permission prior to the assessor coming in for this observation.

**NVQ** Unit 3: 3.1, 3.2, 3.3, 3.4, 5.1, 5.2; Unit 25: 1.3, 2.3; Unit 43: 1.1, 1.3, 3.1, 3.2, 3.3, 4.1, 4.2, 4.3, 5.1, 6.1, 7.7, 7.8 **BTEC** Unit 1: 5.1, 7.1, 7.2, 7.3; Unit 2: 3.1, 3.2, 3.3, 4.1, 4.2, 4.3

## PROFESSIONAL DISCUSSION

Your assessor will carry out a professional discussion with you that will capture the evidence needed to prove your level of knowledge and understanding of topic areas.

Below are some topic areas you will need to think about when preparing for the professional discussion with your assessor:

- Using different office machinery
- Using IT

*Your assessor will plan the content of your professional discussion and will advise you to help you to prepare beforehand. The professional discussion may cover more than this section of your Workbook.*

## Discussion process

The discussion process offers you the chance to show that, as an administrator, you have a good working knowledge of the office equipment in your work area.

To prepare for your professional discussion, you should think about how you could answer questions such as the following:

- How do you make sure work is carried out using office machinery in a timely manner and to the required standards of your organisation?
- What are the different features of office machinery?
- Give reasons why pieces of office equipment are used for various tasks.
- Why is it important to make sure machinery is left in a condition that is fit for use for the next person?
- How do you deal with problems with office machinery?
- Why is it important that work is delivered on time?
- Why is it important to always work to high standards?
- Why is it important to deal with emails in a timely manner?

3

# 3. PREPARING BUSINESS DOCUMENTS

In the previous section, you carried out a series of activities that allowed you to experience a wide range of equipment used in a business organisation. In this section, we look at the production of documents using different resources.

## KNOWLEDGE AND UNDERSTANDING

Being able to produce good, high-quality documents is key to an administrator's role and a task that requires a high degree of skill with IT packages. You must be able to input data accurately and quickly, and make any changes needed. A further important feature is the ability to work with different fonts and styles to produce attractive documents that are fit for purpose. At the same time, you must work within your organisation's guidelines.

In this section, you will follow a series of activities that introduce you to different packages used in businesses for producing documents. After you have you have reviewed these packages, you will be able to make decisions on the best option for each document you have to produce.

As you will see from the diagram below, business documentation is produced for many different reasons.

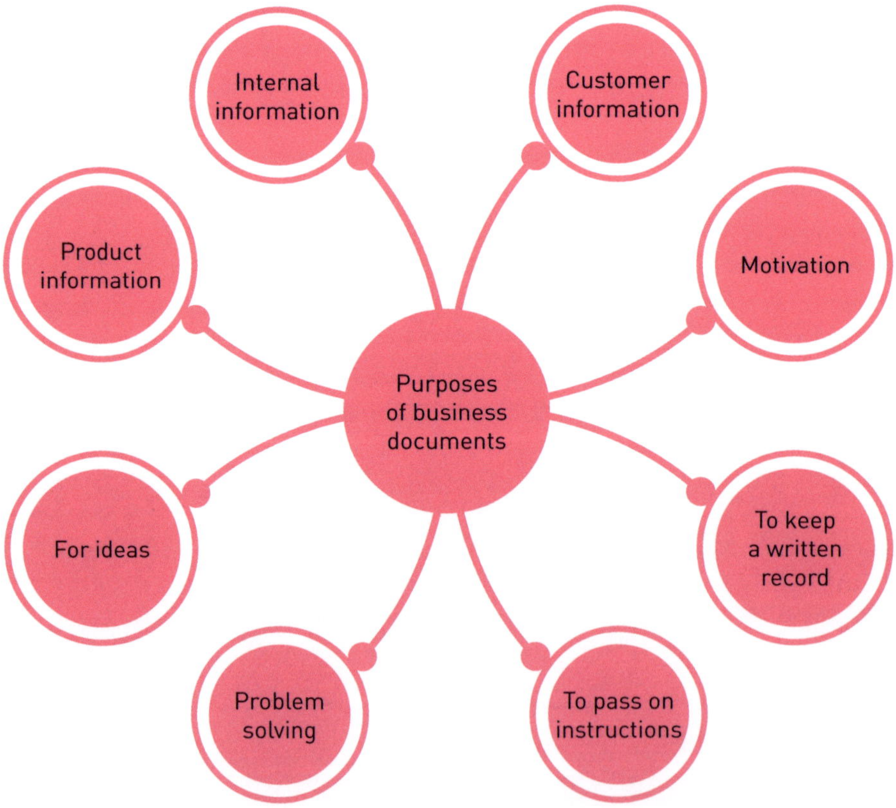


*Can you think of any other reasons why businesses might need documentation?*

**NVQ** Unit 8: 1.1, 2.1, 5.1, 5.4, 5.8

## Task 1

Your organisation may have rules and regulations about the fonts, styles and colours you can use when producing documentation that will be sent to external customers. There may be guidance on the use of the company logo on stationery, as well as other stationery that must be used at all times.

Find your organisational procedures/policies/guidelines on the use of documentation.

You should also find a copy of the following stationery for your organisation:

- letterhead
- compliment slip
- business card
- invoice
- fax header page.

**BTEC** Unit 3: 3.2
**NVQ** Unit 8:1.1

## Task 2

All documentation created in a business organisation is created for a reason and purpose.

The table below lists some documents that you may come across in your role as an administrator. Complete the table, giving the purpose of the document, to whom the document is usually sent and the features of the document. The first line has been completed for you.

| Document | Purpose | Sent to | Features and other comments |
|---|---|---|---|
| Business letter | To inform and communicate with the person receiving it | • External customers/ stakeholders<br>• Employees of the company (possibly via HR) | • Produced on company letterhead with the logo, font and style created as per company policy<br>• Can be a slower form of communication if sent by post, but can be emailed if the letter needs to arrive more quickly<br>• Can be impersonal but also provides a written record |
| Email | | | |

| Document | Purpose | Sent to | Features and other comments |
|---|---|---|---|
| Fax | | | |
| Form – for example, stationery requisition form, or expenses form | | | |
| Informal report | | | |
| Formal report | | | |
| Memo | | | |

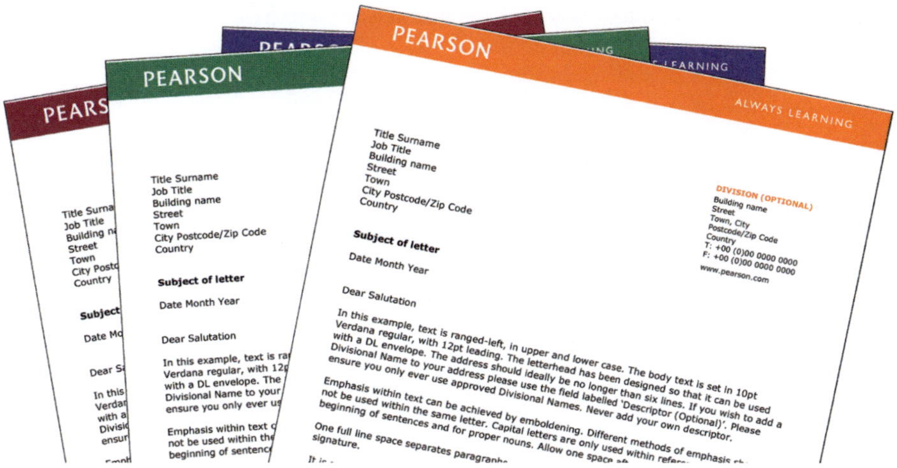


*Which type of headed stationery do you use most frequently in your role?*

**BTEC** Unit 3: 4.2, 4.5
**NVQ** Unit 4: 2.3, 2.4, 2.5, 2.6, 2.8; Unit 8: 1.3

## Task 3

In your role as administrator, there are times when you will be the person making the final decision about how a business document will look when completed.

Read the following scenario:

> *Your line manager has hand-written a letter of reply to a complaint for you to type up in the correct format and post, signing the letter on their behalf. You need to make sure that grammar and spelling are accurate, and that the letter is in the post that evening in time for first-class delivery.*

1. In the table below (which continues on page 56), list the key points to think about when preparing this letter. You must include decisions about language, layout style, font and proofreading. The first line has been completed for you.

| Option | Purpose |
|---|---|
| Choice of layout | • To follow company style<br>• To look professional<br>• To be easily read by the person receiving it |
| | |

| Option | Purpose |
| --- | --- |
| | |
| | |
| | |
| | |
| | |

2. Why do you think it is important to produce high-quality documentation at all times?

   Write your answer in the space below.

**BTEC** Unit 3: 3.1, 4.4
**NVQ** Unit 8: 1.2, 2.1, 2.2, 2.3, 5.10

## Task 4

Your organisation uses many different types of document to produce information for both internal and external use. The list below (which continues on page 58) contains some documents you may produce in your day-to-day work. In the space provided, fill in the correct resource to produce this document and give your reasons. The first line has been completed for you.

| Document | Resource/software needed | Reasons for this choice |
|---|---|---|
| Sales figures – information giving details of sales for the month, with totals and commissions payable | Excel spreadsheet | • Package allows for calculations to be inserted<br>• This package should be used when making lists<br>• Ability to sort for information<br>• Ability to create sub-totals of information in the spreadsheet<br>• Ability to summarise information |
| Letter replying to a complaint | | |
| Company product information brochure | | |
| Letter to multiple external customers | | |
| Presentation to the Board, including graphs and pictures | | |
| Report for the managers' meeting | | |
| Database of customer sales information | | |

| Document | Resource/software needed | Reasons for this choice |
|---|---|---|
| Minutes of meeting | | |
| Internal telephone numbers list | | |

**BTEC** Unit 3: 4.3
**NVQ** Unit 8: 3.5; Unit 4: 2.10

## Task 5

It is important when you prepare documentation within your organisation that you store this information securely and safely. You must also comply with the data protection procedures in place in your organisation.

1. In the first part of this task, use the space below to describe how you save documentation securely on your PC, and how you deal with very confidential documentation. For example, whether you password-protect any data.

2. Why is it important to comply with your organisation's data protection policies and procedures? Write your answer in the space below.

## EVIDENCE GATHERING

In this activity you will identify an area of your work that will capture evidence of how you operate as an administrator. *Your assessor will help you to identify suitable items of evidence.*

You need to gather evidence of activity in areas of your work to demonstrate:

**NVQ** Unit 4: 6.2, 6.3, 6.4; Unit 8: 1.1, 2.3, 3.2, 3.3, 5.1, 5.2, 5.3, 5.4, 5.5, 5.6, 5.7, 5.8

Documentation you have produced using different software packages, demonstrating how you have produced high-quality materials that are fit for purpose.

Suggested evidence may include:

- copies of letters/reports/memos, etc., you have produced
- witness statements
- written evidence from candidate
- screen prints of saved documentation.

**BTEC** Unit 1: 4.1; Unit 3: 4.1, 4.3
**NVQ** Unit 4: 2.7, 2.9; Unit 8: 3.1, 3.4, 3.5, 3.6, 3.7

## PROFESSIONAL DISCUSSION

Your assessor will carry out a professional discussion with you that will capture the evidence needed to prove your level of knowledge and understanding of topic areas.

Below are some topic areas you will need to think about when preparing for the professional discussion with your assessor:

- Standards of work
- Meeting deadlines when completing work
- How you ensure accuracy, including using proofreading tools on your computer
- Storing documents and confidentiality

*Your assessor will plan the content of your professional discussion and will advise you to help you to prepare beforehand. The professional discussion may cover more than this section of your Workbook.*

### Discussion process

The discussion process offers you the chance to show that in your role as administrator, you are able to produce high-quality documents to tight deadlines that are both accurate and grammatically correct. You must also be aware of confidentiality issues around some documents within your organisation, and know how to deal with these.

To prepare for your professional discussion, you should think about how you could answer questions such as the following:

- Why is it important to agree the standard of the work expected with your line manager/colleagues?
- What are the key points to think about when producing documents in terms of layout, content, etc., and what are the benefits of these?
- How do you make sure at all times that the documents you produce are accurate?
- Explain any confidentiality issues in your organisation and how you deal with these.
- How do you make sure documents are stored safely and securely?
- How do you work out which tasks are urgent and which are important?

# 4. CARRY OUT RESEARCH EFFECTIVELY

The internet is an excellent source of information and often the first place used to carry out research or searches for information. However, the internet is not the only source of information. This section looks at different ways to research information effectively to make sure that the correct information is found so that it can be used effectively in everyday business.

## KNOWLEDGE AND UNDERSTANDING

As an administrator, you will often be asked by various members of your team or department to find out information. It is important that you are aware of the different sources of information available, including the internet, intranet, books, journals, magazines, and so on. You need to organise your research in such a way that the information you find is meaningful and can be used effectively by those requesting it. It is important that you put information into a search engine accurately and that you remember your organisation's policy/procedures concerning internet usage.

The activities in this section take you through a series of tasks that will help you to use research tools effectively and efficiently.

*What types of information do you need to research in your role?*

**BTEC** Unit 3: 2.2
**NVQ** Unit 36: 2.2, 2.3, 2.4, 2.5, 2.6

## Task 1

For the first part of this task, you need to find a copy of the following workplace document:

- policy/procedure for internet usage.

For the next part of the task, you need to keep a diary/log of all the sources of information you use over the next month. These sources of information can include:

- the internet
- the intranet
- books
- magazines
- journals.

1. Complete the table below – these are suggested headings, you can use your own if you wish. List all the different sources of information you use. For example, if you used a website, make a note of the web address and which pages you visited, for what purpose you visited this site and whether it was useful.

   The first line of the table has been completed for you. You can continue on a separate page if you wish.

| Date | Source of information | Pages visited | Purpose for research | Was this source useful? |
|---|---|---|---|---|
| 3/9/10 | Internet www.easyjet.com | Flight information pages | Research for a flight to Alicante in November | Yes – the pages brought up information I needed and could use and print off |
| | | | | |
| | | | | |
| | | | | |
| | | | | |

2. When you have researched this information for your line manager or colleague, what do you do with this information? How do you organise it so that it is in a readable format?

   Describe how you deal with researched information in the space below.

**BTEC** Unit 3: 2.2
**NVQ** Unit 36: 2.2, 2.3, 2.4, 2.5, 2.6
**WorkSkills** Unit 7: 2.5

## Task 2

Looking back at the information log you created in Task 1, you are now going to think about other ways of finding information. In the table below, make notes about any other ways you could have found the same information (you may need to continue on a separate piece of paper). For example, if you used the internet to look up flights, could you have used another method, such as the telephone, and would this have been as effective?

The first line has been completed for you as an example.

| Source of information | Purpose | Identify a different source for this information | Is this method as effective as the original method? |
|---|---|---|---|
| www.easyjet.com | Flight information | Telephone | No – much slower, not able to print off information, no on-line discounts available |
| | | | |
| | | | |
| | | | |

3

WorkSkills Unit 7: 1.1, 1.2, 1.3, 1.4, 1.5, 2.1, 2.2, 2.4

## Task 3

As an administrator, you will be asked to research many different topics, but one of the most common research requests in a business environment is for travel arrangements.

In this task, you are going to use the internet to research the following:

- flights to Valencia, from an airport no more than 50 miles from your place of work
- the flight should leave on Sunday (any time) and return on Tuesday evening
- accommodation (a place to stay) in Valencia for two nights, for a budget of €150 per night, per room
- car hire from the airport in Valencia to the accommodation for the duration of the stay in Valencia, returning it to the airport before leaving Valencia.

Create a plan of how you will carry out this research. Your plan could look like the one below, or you could create your own.

| Task | Source of information, including website address | Information gained from this source |
|---|---|---|
| | | |
| | | |
| | | |
| | | |
| | | |
| | | |

By following this plan and gathering all your information, you should be able to produce a possible itinerary (travel plan) that shows the following:

- flight times – both outwards and incoming
- costs of flights
- alternative flights from all airports researched
- car hire costs and pick up and drop off points
- accommodation costs of all hotels chosen
- accommodation addresses of chosen hotels.

You should list all the websites you have visited when carrying out this research in a separate section on the itinerary.

**NVQ** Unit 24: 1.7, 2.7; Unit 31: 2.9; Unit 36: 2.7; Unit 43: 4.3, 7.6

## Task 4

A number of problems may occur while you are at work. There are times when you will have to deal with problems and resolve them to the best of your ability.

Read the following scenario and in the space on page 66, describe how you would deal with this situation so that everyone is happy with the outcome.

*You work as an administrator for a large multi-national organisation in the Sales Department. The majority of your work is for the Sales Director, but occasionally the Assistant Sales Director and Marketing Director ask you to carry out tasks. When setting priorities, you normally put your boss first, and then work on a first-come, first-served basis if anyone else needs you to do something.*

*However, on Thursday morning, the following tasks arrive in your in-tray:*

- *Your boss has asked for the Monthly Sales Report, along with the accompanying sales figures, to be completed by Thursday evening, at the latest, so that he can take the report to a meeting on Friday afternoon.*
- *Your boss has also asked you to begin researching venues for the Sales Department conference, to be held in the spring, and wants to take details of possible venues to the meeting on Friday afternoon.*
- *The Assistant Sales Director has left instructions for you to type and distribute a letter to go out to customers giving details of new products being launched very soon. He is targeting approximately 400 customers. This work needs to be completed no later than Monday afternoon and you need to arrange some help to put the letters into envelopes.*

- *The Marketing Director has asked you to organise meetings for next week and would like the confirmations to go out this afternoon.*

1. In the space below, describe how you would set priorities against each of these tasks, how you would negotiate with each person to make sure all work gets completed and how you would agree new deadlines, where necessary.

2. In the table below, describe the problems that you have met at work so far. These could include a clash of work priorities with colleagues or line managers, or they could be problems associated with customers. You also need to give details on how you managed to solve these problems successfully.

| Describe a problem you have met at work | How did you successfully solve this problem? | For whom was this problem resolved? |
|---|---|---|
| | | |
| | | |
| | | |
| | | |

**BTEC** Unit 1: 7.1, 7.2, 7.3; Unit 3: 2.1
**NVQ** Unit 36: 1.1, 1.2, 1.3; Unit 31: 2.9; Unit 24: 1.7, 2.7; Unit 43: 4.3

## PROFESSIONAL DISCUSSION

Your assessor will carry out a professional discussion with you that will capture the evidence needed to prove your level of knowledge and understanding of topic areas.

Below are some topic areas you will need to think about when preparing for the professional discussion with your assessor:

- Information research
- Dealing with problems

*Your assessor will plan the content of your professional discussion and will advise you to help you to prepare beforehand. The professional discussion may cover more than this section of your Workbook.*

## Discussion process

The discussion process offers you the chance to show that you can negotiate with your colleagues in the workplace to make sure that work is carried out to agreed timescales and deadlines. It will also show that you can search quickly and accurately for information when asked to do so.

To prepare for your professional discussion, you should think about how you could answer questions such as the following:

- Why is it important to agree objectives and deadlines with colleagues when carrying out research projects?
- What are the main reasons why you need to identify and agree the sources of information you are to use for a research project?
- Why do you think it is important to store and record information you have found?
- How do you deal with problems that arise in your working environment?
- How do you decide whether to involve another colleague/line manager when problems arise in the workplace?

# 5. ARCHIVING AND STORAGE

Archiving and storing information in any business is extremely important given that there is rarely space to store files and boxes in modern offices. Archived information must be stored in such a way that you can easily get it back if you need to. Usually you will have to follow strict organisational guidelines to make sure information is not mislaid. Administration staff are normally the key contacts for information that is no longer required but needs to be kept. In the following activities you will look at different types of archiving and storage facilities and think about the legal issues surrounding such information.

## KNOWLEDGE AND UNDERSTANDING

It is important in an office environment, where information is stored and archived for future use that it is stored in such a way that it can be got back very quickly when members of staff need it. Organisational procedures must be followed to make sure that staff follow guidelines when storing and archiving information. Legal issues about storing information must be taken into account where they apply.

There is more to storing information than just locking it away in a cabinet. The information must be stored in good condition, filed in a useable and recognisable order using the correct resources, and stored in lockable cabinets. If electronic systems for storing data are used, then these should be backed up regularly to make sure that no information is lost.

Eventually, the storage areas will need to be cleared and information that is considered to be out of date will need to be either got rid of or archived. Many organisations archive away from the main site, but very often archives are in basements or unused office areas in the building.

**NVQ** Unit 37: 2.2

### Task 1

You may find that your organisation only allows storage and archiving of information in particular places to make sure of confidentiality and security. To make sure that you are working to the correct organisational procedures, find the following guidelines, policies or procedures for your organisation/department about:

- storage of information
- archiving of information
- how your organisation deals with the key elements of the Data Protection Act.

**NVQ** Unit 37: 1.2, 2.3; Unit 38: 1.9

## Task 2

There are many different types of storage that organisations can use to store their information. Your organisation will use different types of storage equipment to make sure that data is stored securely and is easy to find. Remember that storage can be electronic as well as manual.

1. Which types of storage equipment does your organisation use?

_______________________________________________

_______________________________________________

_______________________________________________

_______________________________________________

_______________________________________________

_______________________________________________

_______________________________________________

2. The following images show various types of electronic storage devices that may be used in a business environment. In the space provided below, identify each one and give two purposes for its use. Then make a comment on security and confidentiality issues in relation to each device.

| | |
|---|---|
|  | Purpose:<br>1.<br><br>2.<br><br>Security and confidentiality issues: |
|  | Purpose:<br>1.<br><br>2.<br><br>Security and confidentiality issues: |

| | |
|---|---|
|  | Purpose:<br>1.<br><br>2.<br><br>Security and confidentiality issues: |
|  | Purpose:<br>1.<br><br>2.<br><br>Security and confidentiality issues: |

3. List any other electronic storage devices you can think of in the space below.

**BTEC** Unit 3: 2.3
**NVQ** Unit 37: 1.3, 1.4, 3.2; Unit 38: 1.3, 1.6, 1.8, 2.1, 2.2, 2.3

## Task 3

Read the following scenario and in the space provided describe how:

- you would file the most up-to-date documents
- you would make sure that the most up-to-date documents are filed
- you would deal with those documents that needed to be archived
- you would index the documents

- and where you would store the documents
- you would make sure of the confidentiality and security of the documents
- you would deal with any problems you might meet
- you would stick to procedures.

*You work as an administration assistant in a busy office in the Adult Education Office of the local council. At the end of each academic year, course files need to be dealt with. These files have confidential information about students in them, including their personal information and their achievements over their years of study. The files also have registers and other legal documentation, including risk assessments and health and safety checks, which the council must keep.*

*The major tasks with this work are:*

- *The course files for each course that has been taught during the previous year have to be audited and then filed securely. This usually happens in June.*
- *At the start of the next academic year, new files need to be made in the large upright filing cabinet, one file for each course. This usually happens in August.*
- *Course files that are two years old, or older, need to be prepared to be sent to the archive. The council uses an outside provider for this and each file needs to be packed into specific boxes that must each weigh no more than 15 kgs. This usually happens from September onwards and the archiving company sets a deadline for collection, usually around the end of October, but this can be negotiable.*
- *Files that are more than five years old can be got back from the archive and you must then arrange for them to be destroyed securely.*

## EVIDENCE GATHERING

In this activity you will identify an area of your work that will capture evidence of how you operate as an administrator. *Your assessor will help you to identify suitable items of evidence.*

You need to gather evidence of activity in areas of your work to demonstrate:

**NVQ** Unit 37: 1.4, 1.5, 2.1, 2.2, 2.3, 2.4, 2.5, 2.6, 3.1, 3.2, 3.3, 3.4; Unit 38: 1.3, 1.6, 1.7, 2.1, 2.2, 2.3, 2.4, 2.5, 2.6, 2.7, 2.8, 2.9

Storing data electronically.

Suggested evidence may include:

- witness statements
- screen prints showing where files are stored and maintenance of those files
- written report on how to save files electronically in line with organisational procedures.

**NVQ** Unit 37: 1.4, 1.5, 1.9, 2.1, 2.2, 2.3, 2.4, 2.5, 2.6, 3.1, 3.2, 3.3, 3.4, 3.5, 3.6; Unit 38: 1.3, 1.4, 1.5, 1.6, 1.7, 1.8, 1.9, 1.10, 2.1, 2.2, 2.3, 2.4, 2.5, 2.6, 2.7, 2.8, 2.9

## PUTTING IT INTO PRACTICE

This activity will help your assessor to look at your competence by watching you carrying out workplace activities. This might include asking related questions to test your underpinning knowledge.

Storing data electronically.

The assessor could observe you storing data electronically to an external device, a data management system or on an electronic filing system on your PC. You may wish to provide screen prints of anything that you have saved electronically to show your file structure. Your assessor may ask you why you set up the system in the way that you did. Your assessor will also want to see you successfully get data/information back from your chosen system.

**BTEC** Unit 3: 2.4
**NVQ** Unit 37: 1.1, 1.3, 1.6, 1.7, 1.8; Unit 38: 1.1, 1.2, 1.4, 1.5, 1.7

## PROFESSIONAL DISCUSSION

Your assessor will carry out a professional discussion with you that will capture the evidence needed to prove your level of knowledge and understanding of topic areas.

Below are some topic areas you will need to think about when preparing for the professional discussion with your assessor:

- Archiving documents
- Storage of information

*Your assessor will plan the content of your professional discussion and will advise you to help you to prepare beforehand. The professional discussion may cover more than this section of your Workbook.*

## Discussion process

The discussion process offers you the chance to show your ability to file, archive and get documents back in a way that meets both organisational and legal procedures. The questions will help you to demonstrate your understanding of some of the key issues you must think about when carrying out storage and archiving tasks in your role.

To prepare for your professional discussion, you should think about how you could answer questions such as the following:

- What is the purpose of storing and getting back information in your organisation?
- Why is confidentiality critical to managing information effectively?
- How do you make sure of accuracy when storing information?
- How, and with whom, do you agree timescales and formats for storing and archiving information?
- What are the main reasons for archiving information in an organisation?
- How do you agree the correct period for keeping documents in an archive?
- What is the process in your organisation for getting back archived documents?

# 4

**In this section, your assessor will see you at work communicating with a variety of internal and external customers, and finding suitable solutions to workplace problems.**

**In this section you will find a range of activities to help you prepare and gather evidence for your assessment related to the following topics:**

1. Reception services
2. Communicating effectively
3. Dealing with customers
4. Teamwork

This section deals with different types and ways of communicating in a business setting.

This will be the fourth visit from your assessor during your Apprenticeship programme and will focus on how you communicate both in your role and within the business.

Your assessor will want to see you carrying out tasks in your everyday role that are relevant to this section. These tasks can be real or simulated (to the extent that tasks, such as you making a phone call, are scheduled for when your assessor can see you carry it out). You may also be recorded either by video or other electronic equipment carrying out tasks. However, you may need to get permission from colleagues prior to any recording taking place.

4

# 1. RECEPTION SERVICES

The receptionist is very often a visitor's first contact with an organisation and many first impressions about the business are made at this point. It is important that the receptionist gives a positive image of the company and is helpful and friendly, while at the same time able to deal with quite complex problems.

## KNOWLEDGE AND UNDERSTANDING

The role of the receptionist is very important. The experience that visitors have when they enter the reception area often determines whether or not business takes place, and whether or not your business is recommended.

As a receptionist, you have a responsible position. You are able to influence visitors' opinions of the organisation and you have the ability to promote your business through your actions.

In this section, you will complete a series of activities that will allow you to explore the role of the receptionist and the part it plays in promoting the business. You will also look at how telephone calls are made in line with your organisation's procedures, and at passing messages to colleagues in a timely manner.

**BTEC** Unit 2: 9.1
**NVQ** Unit 31: 1.1

### Task 1

The role of the receptionist is key to the success of the organisation. The role is wide and varied and includes tasks such as meeting and greeting visitors, dealing with queries and answering the telephone.

In the space below, describe what you think the role of the receptionist is and, in particular, focus on the role as a first point of contact for any visitor to the organisation.

**BTEC** Unit 2: 1.2
**NVQ** Unit 24: 1.1, 1.4, 1.9, 1.10, 2.1, 2.4, 2.8, 2.9

## Task 2

4

In this task, you will prepare and make a presentation to your assessor and line manager on the use of the telephone system in your organisation. There is no need to make a PowerPoint presentation. However, you will need to make some notes.

Before you begin this presentation, find a copy of the following workplace documents:

- policy/procedure/guidelines for use of the telephone.

Your oral presentation should include the following points and you should add other points you think are important when using the telephone:

- why it is important to follow company procedures when using the telephone
- the different types of telephone systems and how to use them
- how you would deal with faults in the telephone system
- how you deal with incoming and outgoing calls
- confidentiality issues about telephone calls.

Your presentation should last approximately six minutes.

*What should you think about when answering the phone?*

4

**BTEC** Unit 2: 1.2
**NVQ** Unit 24: 1.3, 2.5, 3.2, 3.4, 4.5, 4.6, 4.7; Unit 31: 4.2

## Task 3

While you are working on reception, it is important that you are able to take messages from callers, and pass messages on to the relevant members of the organisation in a timely manner. You will also need to transfer calls to different members of the organisation, making sure that the information you receive and give out is accurate.

1. Read the following scenarios, and then in the space below, describe how you would deal with these situations.

*You are working on reception for a large training organisation.*

1. *You receive an external call from a very important customer who wants to speak to the training manager. You transfer the call, but the call comes back to you because the training manager is not available. At the same time, you are dealing with another visitor. What do you do?*
2. *A member of the IT training team has asked you to contact the British Computer Society to obtain details of a new qualification. They do not have a number for this organisation. What would you do?*
3. *The administration manager has asked you to call your local college to find out about a range of qualifications they are offering, and how much they are charging. She has given you the number and the name of the person to contact. How would you deal with this request?*

| | |
|---|---|
| 1. | |
| 2. | |
| 3. | |

2. In the table below, you are going to make a log to record all calls you make and receive in your daily work routine. These calls can be internal or external.

   Make a note of each call, the time of the call and the time taken to deal with the issue. Include the topic of the call and describe any problems you met.

   You can use the template below, or you can devise your own template if you want to.

| Date | Time of call | Time taken on call | Person called – external or internal? | Topic of call | Description of any problems met |
|---|---|---|---|---|---|
| | | | | | |
| | | | | | |
| | | | | | |
| | | | | | |
| | | | | | |
| | | | | | |
| | | | | | |
| | | | | | |
| | | | | | |
| | | | | | |
| | | | | | |
| | | | | | |

**BTEC** Unit 2: 9.3
**NVQ** Unit 31: 2.3, 2.4, 4.3

## Task 4

To help you complete this task, you will need to find a copy of the following document(s) from your organisation:

- the policy/procedure for dealing with visitors
- health and safety in the reception area.

**WorkSkills**
Unit 8: 1.1/2.1, 2.4, 2.2
Unit 9: 1.1, 1.6, 1.5
**PLTS** TW: 1, 3, 4, 5
SM: 1, 2, 3, 7

In the space provided below, you are going to create a flow chart that shows the steps taken when a visitor comes to your organisation. You need to include everything that occurs from the moment a visitor steps inside the building, until they leave it.

Write your answer in the space below, or you can use a separate piece of paper if you need to.

## EVIDENCE GATHERING

In this activity you will identify an area of your work that will capture evidence of how you operate in a business administration role. *Your assessor will help you to identify suitable items of evidence.*

You need to gather evidence of activity in areas of your work to demonstrate:

**NVQ** Unit 3: 7.2; Unit 4: 7.1, 7.3, 7.4, 7.5; Unit 6: 7.2, 7.3; Unit 24: 3.1, 3.2, 3.3, 3.4, 3.6, 4.1, 4.3, 4.4, 4.5, 4.6, 4.7; Unit 31: 4.1, 4.2; Unit 34: 7.2

a. Making and receiving telephone calls.

Suggested evidence may include:

- witness statements
- a log of calls made and received
- a written report on how to make and receive calls in your organisation
- recordings of calls from your organisation's telephone system.

**NVQ** Unit 31: 2.3, 4.2, 4.3, 4.4

b. Meeting and greeting visitors to your organisation and making sure that company procedures are followed.

Suggested evidence may include:

- witness statement
- copy of the visitors' log
- written evidence on how to deal with visitors.

**NVQ** Unit 4: 4.1, 7.3, 7.4, 7.5, 8.1; Unit 24: 3.1, 3.2, 3.3, 3.4, 3.5, 3.6, 3.7, 4.1, 4.2, 4.3, 4.4, 4.5, 4.6, 4.7, 4.8; Unit 31: 4.1, 4.2; Unit 34: 8.1, 8.2, 8.3, 9.1; Unit 43 1.2

## PUTTING IT INTO PRACTICE

This activity will help your assessor to assess your competence by watching you carry out workplace activities. This might include asking related questions to test your underpinning knowledge.

a. Making and receiving telephone calls.

Your assessor will want to see how you deal with both incoming and outgoing telephone calls. They will want to see that you are sticking to your organisation's policy and procedure and that the information you give to callers is accurate. They will also want to see that you handle calls effectively when transferring and taking messages from both external and internal callers. The assessor may ask questions about your organisational procedure/policy and ask you why it is important to follow this procedure/policy.

b. Meeting and greeting visitors in reception.

Your assessor will watch you meeting and greeting visitors when they arrive in reception. The assessor will want to see how you deal with the visitors' requirements, and with any problems that arise. The assessor will also want to see how you stick to company policy in respect of health and safety, and security and emergency procedures while visitors are on site. The assessor may ask questions to check your understanding of the company policies and procedures in respect of health and safety, and security.

**BTEC** Unit 2: 9.3
**NVQ** Unit 3: 2.1, 2.2, 2.3, 2.4; Unit 4: 1.1, 3.1, 3.4; Unit 6:1.4, 1.6, 1.7; Unit 24:1.2, 1.6,1.8, 2.2, 2.3, 2.6; Unit 31: 3.1, 3.2, 4.10

## PROFESSIONAL DISCUSSION

Your assessor will carry out a professional discussion with you that will capture the evidence needed to prove your level of knowledge and understanding of topic areas.

Below are some topic areas you will need to think about when preparing for the professional discussion with your assessor:

- The purpose of telephone calls
- Summarising telephone calls
- Communication structures
- Confidentiality and telephone calls
- Other duties of a receptionist

*Your assessor will plan the content of your professional discussion and will advise you to help you to prepare beforehand. The professional discussion may cover more than this section of your Workbook.*

### Discussion process

The discussion process offers you the chance to show that you are comfortable working on reception and have a grasp of the issues that may arise while working in that area.

To prepare for your professional discussion, you should think about how you could answer questions such as the following:

- Why is it important to know the purpose of a telephone call before you make it?
- Why should you try to summarise a telephone call?
- What is the communication structure in your organisation?
- What are the confidentiality issues around telephone callers and working on a reception desk?
- During a quiet period on reception, what would you do?
- Why should you suggest ideas for improving the reception area?
- Why should you carry out additional duties if necessary?

4

# 2. COMMUNICATING EFFECTIVELY IN THE WORKPLACE

In this section, you will undertake a series of activities that will improve your understanding of communication in the workplace and help you to improve your own communication skills. As an administrator, it is vital that you are able to communicate accurately and concisely with colleagues and external customers to make sure the correct messages are sent out, and that there are no misunderstandings where communication is concerned.

## KNOWLEDGE AND UNDERSTANDING

Communication is a wide and varied subject. This section focuses on communication that is written, verbal or through body language and how these methods are used in a business setting.

In the following activities, you will look at active listening, including what it is, how you can improve your active listening to make sure you understand what is being requested, and how you can respond to it. You will think about how you can summarise information to make sure what you want to say is put across accurately. You will also think about other types of communication, when and where it is appropriate to use them and that you are using the correct type of communication for the people you are communicating with.

**BTEC** Unit 1: 3.3
**NVQ** Unit 4: 3.3, 4.1, 7.3, 8.1, 8.2

### Task 1

The picture on the left shows a group engaged in active listening.

1. In the space provided, describe what you think it means to listen actively, and what effect it has on a group.

4

2. What does the following picture tell you? Are the people in the picture actively listening? Write your response in the space provided below.

3. In the space below, you are going to think about and note a time when you actively listened to a person or group. For example, a team meeting you took part in, or a discussion with a colleague or colleagues on how to improve a process in your office environment.

You need to write about the following in the space below:

- What did you do in the discussion/meeting that you think was active listening?
- How did you respond to any requests or information received?
- Did you ask any questions?
- How did you receive feedback?
- Did this feedback help you improve your active listening skills?

4

**BTEC** Unit 7: 3.2
**NVQ** Unit 4: 5.1, 6.1, 6.2, 6.3

## Task 2

In your role as an administrator you will often need to gather relevant information and summarise it into a meaningful note, report or message before passing on the information.

Read the following scenario and in the space below, describe the process you would go through to make sure that the information you give is useable and meaningful.

*You work in a further education college and the assistant principal asks you to collate (put together) the contents of a file containing evidence for a forthcoming inspection. She gives you a list of information she wants you to include in the file, and asks you to index the file and put it in a central place. She asks you to write a brief summary page at the beginning of the file so that colleagues will know what information is held in the file (this should be no more than half a page) and to let colleagues know where the file will be kept.*

You need to think about:

- how you will index the file – what resources will you use?
- how you will compile a short summary – what information should it contain?
- how you will let colleagues know that the file exists and where it is – what would be the most appropriate form of communication method to use?

4

**BTEC** Unit 1: 3.1
**NVQ** Unit 4: 1.3, 1.4

## Task 3

In the following activity, you will need to think about different types of body language communication, and the most appropriate times to use them.

Look at the pictures below of different types of communication using body language. In the space provided, state whether each picture shows a negative or positive image, and when you would (or wouldn't) use these forms of communication. Give a reason for each answer.

4

NVQ Unit 4: 5.1

## Task 4

What other forms of communication can you think of? Write your answer in the space below, giving reasons why this form of communication is appropriate in a particular situation.

For example, you might like to include written communication in your answer – this is appropriate when a more formal answer to a query is needed.

## EVIDENCE GATHERING

In this activity you will identify an area of your work that will capture evidence of how you operate as an administrator. *Your assessor will help you to identify suitable items of evidence.*

You need to gather evidence of activity in areas of your work to demonstrate:

**BTEC** Unit 7: 3.2
**NVQ** Unit 4: 5.2, 5.3, 6.1, 6.2, 6.7, 6.8

Your written communications.

Suggested evidence may include:

- diary or log of written communications
- witness statements
- letters, emails, memos, etc.

**BTEC** Unit 1: 3.1
**NVQ** Unit 4: 3.2, 3.3, 4.1, 7.1, 7.2, 7.3, 7.4, 7.5, 8.1, 8.2

## PUTTING IT INTO PRACTICE

This activity will help your assessor to assess your competence by watching you carry out workplace activities. This might include asking related questions to test your underpinning knowledge.

Communicating effectively with a colleague, line manager or customer.

Your assessor will want to see how you communicate with people at all levels of the organisation, and also with external customers. You may want to set up a meeting between yourself, your line manager and assessor to discuss your progress, during which time you can actively take part in this discussion. Your assessor may ask you questions about communication within your organisation and the impact it has on your work as an administrator.

**BTEC** Unit 1: 3.1, 3.2, 3.3
**NVQ** Unit 4: 1.1, 1.2, 2.1, 3.4, 4.2; Unit 8: 3.1; Unit 24: 1.2; Unit 25; 1.5; Unit 31: 2.1, 2.2

## PROFESSIONAL DISCUSSION

Your assessor will carry out a professional discussion with you, that will capture the evidence needed to prove your level of knowledge and understanding of topic areas.

Below are some topic areas you will need to think about when preparing for the professional discussion with your assessor:

- The purpose of communication
- Identifying the audience
- Active listening
- Feedback
- Communication structures

*Your assessor will plan the content of your professional discussion and will advise you to help you to prepare beforehand. The professional discussion may cover more than this section of your Workbook.*

## Discussion process

The discussion process offers you the chance to show that you understand how communication impacts on your organisation, and particularly in your role. As an administrator, you will be exposed to different kinds of communication every day, so it is important that you are aware of the different types, and know how to deal with them.

To prepare for your professional discussion, you should think about how you could answer questions such as the following:

- What is the purpose of communication?
- Why is it important to know your audience before communicating?
- What is active listening and why is it important?
- How important is feedback in communication?
- What is the communication structure of your organisation?
- How does this communication structure impact on your role?

4

# 3. DEALING WITH CUSTOMERS

As an administrator, one of your key roles is to support both your internal customers (colleagues) and external customers (those who visit the company or contact it by telephone). The level of support you give varies between different organisations, but on a daily basis, the majority of customers you will come into contact with will be internal. Both types of customer are important and you will be introduced to both in this section.

## KNOWLEDGE AND UNDERSTANDING

The following tasks take you through a series of short activities relating to identifying and dealing with different types of customers and their needs.

It is extremely important for you in your role to understand and identify what customer expectations are, how they can be met and, if possible, exceeded. This will make sure that your customers remain happy with the service you have provided. You also need to identify potential problems and how you can resolve them satisfactorily, again to make sure that customer expectations are met and exceeded.

*It is sometimes difficult to meet the needs of several customers at the same time!*

**BTEC** Unit 2: 8.1
**NVQ** Unit 34: 1.1, 7.1

## Task 1

Before you complete this task, find a copy of your organisation/departmental policy or procedure for dealing with customers.

In the space below, describe who you think are:

- internal customers – give names of who you think your internal customers are
- external customers – give an example of who you deal with externally.

1. Internal customers:

2. External customers:

**NVQ** Unit 34: 2.1

## Task 2

Having identified the differences between internal and external customers, in the space below describe the following:

- the type of service(s) you provide in your role to both external and internal customers
- how you make sure customers' expectations are met.

1. Describe the service you give in your role:

2. How are customers' expectations met?

**BTEC** Unit 2: 8.3, 8.4; Unit 7: 3.2, 3.4
**NVQ** Unit 34: 5.1, 5.3

## Task 3

Read the following scenario and follow the instructions to complete the task.

> *You work as a receptionist in a large hotel chain in a major city in the UK. The majority of the hotel clients are businessmen/women on short stays and many came from all over the world. It is your job to deal with check-in and check-out procedures, give information to clients and answer general queries.*

How would you deal with the following situations? Give your answers in the space provided:

| | | |
|---|---|---|
| 1. | A large queue is forming at the check-in desk. What would you do? | |
| 2. | You are dealing with a businessman whose English is limited. How would you handle this? | |
| 3. | A German tourist is asking for directions to the local theatre. What information would you give them? | |
| 4. | A guest has come to reception to report a problem with the lights in their room. What would you do? | |

| | | |
|---|---|---|
| 5. | A guest has rung down for room service. What would you do? | |
| 6. | The telephone rings while you are on reception and a potential customer is asking about rates for booking a meeting room. How would you handle the call? | |
| 7. | A meeting room is not quite ready for a large group and they are complaining to you about the delay. How would you handle this situation? | |
| 8. | You are having trouble finding a booking that a guest has made. What would you do? | |
| 9. | A double booking has taken place and you need to find alternative accommodation for the guest. What would you say to the guest? | |
| 10. | You have received a compliment from a guest. How would you handle this? | |

**NVQ** Unit 34: 10.1

## Task 4

Collecting customer feedback is a vital part of good customer service if your organisation is to continually improve.

Thinking of your own role in your organisation, and of the customers you deal with, you are going to design a questionnaire that will capture information you can use to improve your own and your department's service to your customers. You will need to work with your line manager/supervisor to carry out this task, as you may need permission to contact external customers. Your line manager/supervisor may also have ideas about the questions they would want to ask.

This questionnaire should be aimed at both internal and external customers.

In the space below, make some brainstorming-style notes of the possible questions you will ask your customers.

Prepare your questionnaire, based on the notes you have made above, using a word-processing or other suitable software package.

**NVQ** Unit 34: 6.1, 6.3, 10.2, 10.3

## Task 5

Once you have designed your questionnaire, think about the following questions and complete the table by providing your answers.

| | Issue to think about | Your response |
|---|---|---|
| 1. | Why is it important to monitor customer comments? | |
| 2. | Why is it important to always improve your service? | |

4

| | Issue to think about | Your response |
|---|---|---|
| 3. | How would you deal with customer complaints? | |
| 4. | How would you publicise the results of your questionnaire? | |
| 5. | How do you make sure customer expectations are always met? | |

**BTEC** Unit 7: 2.2, 3.1, 3.3
**NVQ** Unit 6: 7.3; Unit 34: 5.4, 7.2, 7.3, 7.4, 8.1, 8.2, 8.3, 9.1

## PUTTING IT INTO PRACTICE

This activity will help your assessor to assess your competence by watching you carry out workplace activities. This might include asking related questions to test your underpinning knowledge.

Dealing with internal and external customers' general queries.

Your assessor will want to see you dealing with both internal and external customers in your day-to-day role. This could include dealing with external customers at reception or on the phone. Internal customers could simply be colleagues asking you to carry out tasks as part of your role. The assessor may ask you questions during this observation to make sure that you are meeting expectations and working to company guidelines.

**BTEC** Unit 2: 8.2; Unit 7: 1.2, 2.1, 2.2, 3.3
**NVQ** Unit 34: 3.1, 3.2, 3.3, 3.4, 4.1, 4.2, 4.3, 5.2, 5.4, 6.2

## PROFESSIONAL DISCUSSION

Your assessor will carry out a professional discussion with you that will capture the evidence needed to prove your level of knowledge and understanding of topic areas.

Below are some topic areas you will need to think about when preparing for the professional discussion with your assessor:

- Company procedures in relation to dealing with customers
- Customer needs and expectations
- Positive working relationships

*Your assessor will plan the content of your professional discussion and will advise you to help you to prepare beforehand. The professional discussion may cover more than this section of your Workbook.*

## Discussion process

The discussion process offers you the chance to show how you deal with both internal and external customers in your daily role, how you make sure that expectations are met and exceeded, and how you promote positive working relationships with all customers.

To prepare for your professional discussion, you should think about how you could answer questions such as the following:

- Why is it important to follow company procedures when dealing with customer complaints?
- How do you make sure that customer needs and expectations are met?
- How can you make sure that customer expectations are exceeded?
- What do you think would happen if customer expectations were not met?
- How do you make sure that you keep a positive relationship with all your colleagues?
- What is the benefit of having a positive relationship with customers?

4

# 4. TEAMWORK

*Teamwork can be very productive.*

> *Team means: Together Everyone Achieves More! – Author Unknown*
>
> *Individual commitment to a group effort – that is what makes a team work, a company work, a society work, a civilization work. – Vince Lombardi*

There are many different quotes and sayings about teamwork, but it is without doubt one of the most important aspects of working in a busy business environment. Although the role of an administrator can be isolating at times, there are many occasions where working as part of a larger team can be not only rewarding, but can also be motivating, so that work is completed much more quickly and efficiently. It is a great strength of any administrator to be able to move from working individually to being a competent member of a team.

## KNOWLEDGE AND UNDERSTANDING

The activities in this section will take you through the purpose of team working, and help you understand when a team situation can be beneficial to a particular project or piece of work. The activities allow you to identify when working in a team would be beneficial to you and how you can contribute effectively to that team environment.

It is important for teams to have goals and objectives so that all members know what they are working towards. There also needs to be respect for each member of the team, and recognition of the different strengths each person can bring to the team.

In team situations, there will be issues to resolve, and differences of opinion that need to be worked through. The following activities will give you an insight as to how this can be achieved.

**NVQ** Unit 6: 2.2, 6.2
**WorkSkills:** Unit 8: 1.1, 1.2, 1.3
**PLTS** EP: 1, 2, 3, 4, 5
TW: 1, 2, 3, 5, 6

## Task 1

In this activity, you are going to undertake a group task. This task could be with fellow administrators in your department/organisation, with colleagues in your department or with members of your class.

First of all, you need to:

- identify a suitable task
- set goals and objectives for this task
- identify strengths of other members of the team.

Following the above, you then need to:

- decide what role each of you has in the team
- think about how you are going to adapt your behaviour while working as part of the team
- give feedback to, and receive feedback from, the team during the task
- on completion, reflect on how you could have improved your performance.

1. You should write your responses in the space below.

4

2. In the space below, describe what might happen if a team member did not perform as well as they should, or did not follow the code of conduct set by the group.

**NVQ** Unit 1: 3.3, 4.5, Unit 6: 2.4, 2.5, 3.2, 4.1, 5.1, 5.2, 8.1, 8.4, 8.6, 9.1, 9.2, 9.3, 10.1, 10.2, 10.3
**WorkSkills** Unit 8: 2.1, 2.3, 2.4

## Task 2

Looking back at Task 1, in which you were a member of a team, you now need to think about the following questions about your own performance in the team, and fill in the answers in the space provided.

| | Team issues | Reflections on my responses |
|---|---|---|
| 1. | Did you support other team members during the task? If yes, please state what this support was. | |
| 2. | Did you require any support during the task from members of the team? | |
| 3. | Did the group communicate well with each other? Please state which methods of communication were used. | |
| 4. | Why do you think it was important to recognise the strengths of individual team members? | |
| 5. | Did the team have any problems while working on the task? | |
| 6. | How did you help to resolve any problems? | |
| 7. | Was the task completed on time? | |
| 8. | Did you **receive** feedback from your team members? | |

| | Team issues | Reflections on my responses |
|---|---|---|
| 9. | Did you **give** feedback to any of your team members? | |
| 10. | How could you have improved **your** performance in the team? | |

**NVQ:** Unit 1: 4.5; Unit 2: 2.1, 2.2, 2.3; Unit 3: 6.1, 6.2; Unit 4: 7.1, 7.2, 7.4; Unit 6: 2.4, 2.5, 2.6, 3.1, 3.2, 4.1, 5.1, 5.2, 8.1, 8.2, 8.3, 8.4, 8.5, 8.6, 9.1, 9.2, 9.3, 10.1, 10.2,10.3
**WorkSkills:** Unit 8: 2.1, 2.2, 2.3

## PUTTING IT INTO PRACTICE

This activity will help your assessor to assess your competence by watching you carry out workplace activities. This might include asking related questions to test your underpinning knowledge.

Participating in your team task.

**WorkSkills** Unit 8: 1.1/2.1, 1.1/1.2/1.3, 1.3/2.2, 2.4, 2.2, 2.3/2.4
**PLTS** TW: 1, 2, 3, 4, 5, 6

The assessor will want to see you taking part in a task during which you are making a full contribution to make sure the task is completed. The assessor will want to see your interaction (how you behave) with other team members, your communication skills, how you deal with conflict and how it is resolved, as well as how objectives and goals are met to make sure the task is completed on time. The assessor may also ask questions about your view of teams, and how they work in your organisation.

**NVQ** Unit 1: 1.3; Unit 2: 1.2: Unit 3: 1.1, 1.2, 1.3, 1.4: Unit 4: 4.1, 4.2; Unit 6: 2.1, 2.3, 2.6, 4.2, 4.3, 6.1,
**WorkSkills** Unit 8: 1.1, 1.2, 1.3
**PLTS** TW: 1, 2, 3
**BTEC** Unit 1: 4.1, 6.1, 6.2

## PROFESSIONAL DISCUSSION

Your assessor will carry out a professional discussion with you that will capture the evidence needed to prove your level of knowledge and understanding of topic areas.

Below are some topic areas you will need to think about when preparing for the professional discussion with your assessor:

- Goals and objectives in team working, and their benefits
- Code of conduct of the team
- Diversity in teams
- Respecting individual team members
- Feedback

*Your assessor will plan the content of your professional discussion and will advise you to help you to prepare beforehand. The professional discussion may cover more than this section of your Workbook.*

## Discussion process

The discussion process offers you the chance to show that you understand the impact (effect) team working can have on an organisation, and on individuals and their effectiveness.

To prepare for your professional discussion, you should think about how you could answer questions such as the following:

- Why is it important that the team sets goals and objectives?
- What are the advantages of agreeing a code of conduct for the team?
- Why is it important for the team to have diverse members?
- How do you make sure of respect for your fellow team members?
- What is the value of receiving and giving feedback on the team's performance?

# 5

**In this section, there are a number of activities relating to equality and diversity and behaviour at work, as well as health and safety at work. In this section, you will also look at sustainability and waste in business.**

**In this section you will find a range of activities to help you prepare and gather evidence for your assessment related to the following topics:**

1. Equality and diversity and behaviour in the workplace
2. Health and safety and sustainability issues in business

As you are following a practical programme, your assessor will probably want to see you in the workplace undertaking some of the activities you carry out on a day-to-day basis. Evidence collected for this set of activities may include reports you have written, witness statements completed by a colleague or line manager/supervisor, or photographs or video. You could also include appraisals, performance reviews or reflective accounts, where appropriate. You may need to get permission before photographs or recordings are taken.

The assessor may wish to meet your line manager or supervisor to tell them about your progress and to make sure you are on track to complete on the agreed date.

5

# 1. EQUALITY AND DIVERSITY AND BEHAVIOUR IN THE WORKPLACE

When working in business administration, you are often the first contact a potential customer has with the business. You therefore need to make sure that you project a positive image (both of the organisation and of yourself). First impressions can determine whether or not a business transaction takes place. As well as creating a good impression, it is also extremely important to treat people fairly and with respect, and it is vital that you are able to follow your organisation's equality and diversity procedures.

## KNOWLEDGE AND UNDERSTANDING

In the following tasks you will carry out activities that help you to identify how a positive image of both yourself and the organisation can be achieved. You will explore what diversity means, and look at how to treat people with respect.

**BTEC** Unit 2: 9.1, 9.2; Unit 7: 1.1
**NVQ** Unit 24: 3.5, 4.2; Unit 31: 4.1

### Task 1

In the following activity, you will look at some images that project either a positive or negative image of yourself or your organisation. You must select the most appropriate image to match the description, and give your reasons why you have chosen it. Use the space provided to write your responses.

1. Which of the following images would project a positive image of you at work?

a.

b.

2. You are working on reception. Which of the images below would give a positive image of the organisation? Give your reasons in the space provided.

a.

b.

5

3. In the space below, describe how you would show a positive image of both yourself and the organisation. You might like to think about how you deal with customers on the telephone, or how you deal with people when you meet them for the first time.

**BTEC** Unit 1: 4.3
**NVQ** Unit 1: 2.7, 4.4

## Task 2

While you are at work, it is important that you treat people with respect and make sure that they are not offended in any way by the way you work, or by what you say. In the following activity, you need to think about how your behaviour at work shows honesty, respect and consideration to others, as well as any behaviours that don't show these qualities. Some positive types of behaviour are listed in the table below. Complete the table with another three examples of actions that show each type of behaviour positively, and three examples of negative actions.

The first line of each section of the table has been completed for you as an example.

| Behaviour | Types of actions that show this behaviour positively | Types of actions that show this behaviour negatively |
|---|---|---|
| Honesty | 1. *Owning up when a mistake happens*<br>2.<br>3.<br>4. | 1. *Lying to cover tracks when a mistake has been made*<br>2.<br>3.<br>4. |
| Respect | 1. *Listening when people are talking*<br>2.<br>3.<br>4. | 1. *Interrupting people when they are talking*<br>2.<br>3.<br>4. |

| Behaviour | Types of actions that show this behaviour positively | Types of actions that show this behaviour negatively |
|---|---|---|
| Consideration towards others | 1. *Complimenting people who have done well*<br>2.<br>3.<br>4. | 1. *Making cruel jokes or comments about people*<br>2.<br>3.<br>4. |

**NVQ** Unit: 3: 1.1, 1.2, 1.3, 6.4

## Task 3

In this activity, you are going to take a closer look at what diversity actually means, and find a definition that describes it. You may find this definition in your organisation's procedure for equality and diversity.

You are also going to look at sensitivity between your colleagues and why it is important to treat people in a way that respects their values, abilities, background, customs and beliefs.

1. In the space below, describe what you think diversity actually is. You could use a dictionary to find out what it means, or you could look in your organisation's procedures for equality and diversity to find out what diversity means to the organisation.

2. Why do you think it is important to value diversity?

3. Look at the following situations that might happen while you are at work. In the space provided, write your response to the questions, and give the reasons for your answers.

| | Scenario | How would you react, what would you do, and why? |
|---|---|---|
| 1. | You have received an email from a friend that contains something you think is hilarious. You want to pass it on to other people in your office.<br><br>What should you do? | |
| 2. | You have been asked to give a short talk to a new member of staff about how people in your organisation treat each other.<br><br>What topics would you include in your talk? | |
| 3. | One of your colleagues in the office is always picking on your friend in another section. Your friend is getting increasingly upset over the comments being made about her, and thinks they are racist, but your colleague just thinks they are funny.<br><br>What should you do? | |
| 4. | A new member of staff has recently joined your organisation, and follows a religion that does not celebrate Christmas. You are about to put up the Christmas decorations in the office.<br><br>How should you deal with this situation? | |

**BTEC** Unit 1: 1.6; Unit 2: 1.3, 9.2; Unit 7: 1.1
**NVQ** Unit 1: 2.5, 2.6; Unit 6: 1.4, 1.6; Unit 24: 1.5; Unit 31: 1.2, 1.3

## PROFESSIONAL DISCUSSION

Your assessor will carry out a professional discussion with you that will capture the evidence needed to prove your level of knowledge and understanding of topic areas.

Below are some topic areas you will need to think about when preparing for the professional discussion with your assessor:

- How you present a positive image of yourself
- How you present a positive image of your organisation
- The impact on potential customers of not presenting a positive image
- The importance of following equality and diversity procedures at work
- The purpose of treating others with honesty, consideration and respect

*Your assessor will plan the content of your professional discussion and will advise you to help you to prepare beforehand. The professional discussion may cover more than this section of your Workbook.*

### Discussion process

The discussion process offers you the chance to show how you treat others in the workplace. It is important to treat other colleagues with respect, honesty and consideration while you are at work, and you should expect the same behaviour in return. Your assessor will also ask you questions about how you make sure that a positive image of both yourself and the organisation is shown. This can happen in many different ways. Your assessor will also look at the impact of *not* showing a positive image.

To prepare for your professional discussion, you should think about how you could answer questions such as the following:

- How can you show a positive image of yourself?
- How can you show a positive image of your organisation?
- Why is it important to show a positive image of both yourself and the organisation?
- What could the impact be of not being positive?
- How do you make sure that all colleagues you come into contact with are treated with consideration, honesty and respect?
- Why is it important that you treat colleagues with consideration, honesty and respect?
- Why is it important to be aware of legislation such as the Equality Act, the Disability Discrimination Act, the Sex Discrimination Act, etc.?

5

# 2. HEALTH AND SAFETY AND SUSTAINABILITY ISSUES IN BUSINESS

It is important that health and safety issues in the workplace are identified and dealt with quickly so that everyone is safe in the office environment. It is the responsibility of everyone in the organisation to identify health and safety issues, and to report anything that they think could cause a hazard. Employee responsibilities also include 'green' issues, the most common one being eliminating waste in the business environment. This section deals with both health and safety and waste reduction topics.

## KNOWLEDGE AND UNDERSTANDING

In the following tasks you will look at health and safety implications in relation to your workstation, and why it is important to follow manufacturers' instructions when operating office equipment. You will also think about how to minimise waste in a business, including dealing with hazardous waste material. Finally, you will think about how to keep confidential documents that are created within the organisation secure, and how to deal with potential conflict in the office.

**BTEC** Unit 1: 2.1, 2.3, Unit 2: 3.3
**NVQ** Unit 52: 1.1, 1.3, 1.4, 2.2, 2.3, 2.4

### Task 1

In this task, you are going to look at health and safety issues concerning your workstation, including the safe way to sit in front of a PC. You will also think about how to care for your workstation and make sure that it is regularly maintained.

*Is this the correct way to sit at a PC?*

1. For the following task, look at the image on page 110 of a person sitting at a desk using a PC. You need to answer the questions in the table below. You may have to do some research to answer some of the questions.

| | **Question** | **Your answer** |
|---|---|---|
| 1. | Is the chair supporting the user's back? | |
| 2. | Do you think the screen is at the correct height for the user? | |
| 3. | Look at the position of the user's hands. Is this the correct position? If not, describe the correct position for hands on the keyboard. | |
| 4. | When using a PC, where should your feet be positioned? | |
| 5. | Where should the document that you are currently using be placed on your desk? | |
| 6. | Where should the mouse be placed on the desk? | |
| 7. | What techniques should you put in place to avoid repetitive strain injury? | |

2. What guidelines are in place in your organisation to make sure that employees use a keyboard safely?

3. What procedures should you follow to make sure that your workstation is cared for and maintained?

4. What do you think are the responsibilities of both employer and employee in relation to health, safety and security in the workplace?

5. How do you make sure that your working environment is safe and secure?

6. Why is it important to make sure that equipment is clean and hygienic for the next user?

7. What techniques can be used to make sure that the user of a keyboard avoids getting repetitive strain syndrome in future years?

5

**BTEC** Unit 2: 3.2
**NVQ** Unit 3: 8.4; Unit 43: 2.1, 2.2, 2.3

## Task 2

The office is full of equipment that is used every day. This machinery must be used safely.

1. In the space below, list all the machinery in your office and identify where you can find the manufacturer's instructions to help you and your colleagues to use the machinery safely. The first line has been completed for you as an example.

| | Office machinery | Location of manufacturer's instructions |
|---|---|---|
| 1. | Fax machine | Directly above the fax machine, pinned to the noticeboard. |
| | | |
| | | |
| | | |

2. Looking at the machinery you have identified in your office, are there any health and safety procedures available in your organisation for using any of these pieces of equipment? If there are, list these in the space below. (You may need to ask your supervisor or line manager for details of where to find these procedures.)

3. Why do you think it is important to follow manufacturer's instructions when operating office machinery? Write your answer in the space below.

**BTEC** Unit 2: 4.1, 4.2, 4.3
**NVQ** Unit 3: 3.1, 3.2, 3.3, 3.4, 3.5, 3.6, 4.1, 4.2, 5.1, 5.2, 8.1, 8.2, 8.3; Unit 43: 3.1, 3.2, 3.3, 7.3

## Task 3

Waste in business is a huge problem and we are now all being asked to minimise waste as much as we can, and to recycle wherever possible.

In these activities, you are going to think about how you can reduce waste, including the steps you can take to make sure that waste is kept to a minimum when you use office machinery. You will also look at technological and hazardous waste, and think about the most efficient way of disposing of it, as well as looking at recycling and how your organisation can benefit from recycling. You will put some of your findings into a presentation for your colleagues and line manager.

1. In the first task, you will look at how you can minimise waste, while still completing work tasks efficiently. Think about how you can use technology to make sure that you minimise waste, then complete the following table with your findings. The first two lines have been completed for you.

5

| Problem | How to overcome it and minimise waste |
|---|---|
| Photocopy paper usage has increased | Set the photocopy machine to automatically print double-sided |
| Too many pages printed from Excel document | Use print preview button to make sure we print only what is necessary |
| | |
| | |
| | |
| | |
| | |
| | |
| | |

2. Create an oral or PowerPoint presentation to deliver to your colleagues and line manager that covers the points listed below. You could make the presentation more interactive by asking your audience questions, such as the ones below, and encouraging their suggestions.
   - Why do you think it is important to keep waste to a minimum?
   - What changes can you make to your working practices to minimise waste? Remember to include the use of technology.
   - What do you think are the benefits of recycling?
   - Why should your organisation recycle?
3. Disposal of hazardous materials must be carried out with great care. Organisations must follow strict procedures to make sure that disposal is safe and doesn't cause harm to people, the environment or in any other ways.

   Complete the following table, giving examples of how your organisation follows procedures to dispose of hazardous and technological waste. The first line has been completed for you as an example of what you should include.

| Waste material | How is waste disposed of?<br>Does your organisation follow a specific procedure? |
|---|---|
| Laser printer cartridges | My organisation arranges for a specialist person to call into the organisation on a monthly basis to collect all used cartridges, so that they can take them away and dispose of them efficiently. Everyone who has a printer must take their used cartridge to the IT department to obtain a replacement cartridge. |
| | |
| | |

4. Finally, looking at the waste generated by your organisation, write a short report on the changes you think could be made to keep waste to a minimum. You can focus only in your own area, especially if you work in a large department or company. However, if you work in a small company, you could take into account everything that happens in the organisation.

**NVQ** Unit 3: 2.1, 2.2, 2.3, 2.4, 7.1, 7.2, 7.3

## Task 4

Organisational security is important – keeping documents and information safe and secure is very important to the integrity of the organisation. In your role as a business administrator, you play a key role in the security of documents in an organisation.

Look at the table on page 119 and list the types of information that might be held by these organisations. Give the reasons why they would hold each type of information. The first line has been completed for you as an example.

1. Name two types of confidential information that the following organisations hold about people:

| Organisation | Confidential information held | Reasons why the information is held |
|---|---|---|
| College of further education | 1. Name and address<br>2. | 1. To be able to send student details of starting dates, and other information, for new courses<br>2. |
| Doctor | 1.<br>2. | 1.<br>2. |
| Solicitor | 1.<br>2. | 1.<br>2. |
| Bank | 1.<br>2. | 1.<br>2. |

2. A new employee in your organisation has found out that several people in the office know confidential information about her, including her date of birth and her mother's maiden name. Her salary also seems to be public knowledge.

   a. How do you think this breach of information could happen in an organisation?

5

b. What steps should the organisation take to make sure that this breach of confidentiality does not happen again?

3. Read the following scenarios and in the space provided, describe what you would do, referring to any organisational procedures you *must* follow in each of these situations.

| **Situation** | **What would you do?** |
|---|---|
| You are walking down a corridor to go to another department and notice a person you do not recognise. They are not wearing a company ID or a visitor's badge. | |
| Your computer starts to run very slowly and then crashes. | |
| You are working on reception when a man walks in who is not wearing a uniform you recognise. He wants to deliver a suspicious-looking parcel. | |
| You are working in HR and a friend of one of your colleagues rings. Your colleague has left the office for the evening. The friend asks you for your colleague's address and telephone number. | |
| It is a very warm day and you want to open a window. The window won't open. | |

NVQ Unit 31: 2.7, 2.8

## Task 5

In this task, you will look at emergency procedures in your organisation and think about situations where conflict may arise at work, particularly with visitors.

Answer the following questions, writing your answer in the space provided.

1. What are the emergency procedures in your organisation, for example if there is a fire? What is your role in this procedure?

2. Working on reception can mean coming into contact with aggressive people who may sometimes cause conflict. What type of incident do you think could contribute to a person becoming aggressive? How would you minimise this aggression and avoid a conflict situation?

**BTEC** Unit 1: 2.2
**NVQ** Unit 31: 2.5, 2.6; Unit 43: 2.3, 2.4, 2.5, 6.1; Unit 52: 1.1, 1.2, 1.3

## PROFESSIONAL DISCUSSION

Your assessor will carry out a professional discussion with you that will capture the evidence needed to prove your level of knowledge and understanding of topic areas.

Below are some topic areas you will need to think about when preparing for the professional discussion with your assessor:

- The purpose of following guidelines about how to use a keyboard
- The purpose of health, safety and security requirements in a business situation
- The purpose of following procedures when using equipment
- Why equipment should be left clean and tidy
- Health and safety procedures about working in reception
- Minimising waste in business

*Your assessor will plan the content of your professional discussion and will advise you to help you to prepare beforehand. The professional discussion may cover more than this section of your Workbook.*

## Discussion process

The discussion process offers you the chance to show that you have an understanding of the health and safety requirements in your sector, and in an office environment. The discussion will focus particularly on the use of machinery and working in different areas of the building.

To prepare for your professional discussion, you should think about how you could answer questions such as the following:

- What is the purpose of guidelines for users of keyboards?
- Why is it important to have health, safety and security procedures in an organisation?
- Why should you follow procedures when using office equipment?
- Why is it important to make sure that equipment is left clean and hygienic for the next user after you have used it?
- How do you make sure that health and safety procedures in reception are implemented?
- Why is it important to have health and safety procedures for reception?
- Why do you think it is important for an organisation to actively try to reduce its waste?